FROM THE
Great War
TO THE
Global Village

A Window on the World

CREDITS

Editor
Peter St. John

Editorial Assistance
Barbara Huck
and Deborah Riley

Design and layout
Dawn Huck

Prepress
Embassy Graphics

Printing
Printcrafters, Manitoba

Copyright © Peter St. John

All rights reserved. The use of any part of this publication reproduced, transmitted in any form or by any means — electronic, photocopying, recording or otherwise — or stored in a retrieval system without the prior written consent of Heartland Associates Inc. (or, in the case of photocopying, without a licence from the Canadian Reprography Collective, CANCOPY) is an infringement of the copyright law.

Library and Archives Canada Cataloguing in Publication

    From the Great war to the global village : a window on the world / edited by Peter St. John.

Includes bibliographical references.
ISBN 1-896150-23-3

    1. Canada--Foreign relations--1945- 2. World politics, 1995-2005.
3. Canadian Institute of International Affairs--History. I. St. John, Peter

FC602.F76 2005   327.71   C2005-902240-X

FROM THE
Great War
TO THE
Global Village

A Window on the World

Edited by Peter St. John

Heartland Associates Inc.
Winnipeg, Canada

Printed in Manitoba, Canada

TABLE OF CONTENTS

7
INTRODUCTION

FROM THE GREAT WAR TO THE GLOBAL VILLAGE

10
PART ONE
JOHN W. DAFOE:
THE WINNIPEG FREE PRESS AND FOREIGN POLICY 1928–1945
Frances Russell

36
PART TWO
FROM THE COLD WAR TO THE NEW WORLD ORDER 1945–2005
Peter St. John

CANADA'S WINDOW ON THE WORLD

54
THE WORLD ACCORDING TO OTTAWA 1986
John Holmes

72
SLOUCHING TOWARD THE MILLENNIUM 1997
Colin Robertson

86
GLOBALIZATION AND THE NATIONAL PROSPECT 1998
Daryl Copeland

98
THE CHALLENGES OF SHARED SECURITY 1999
Christine Shelly

TABLE OF CONTENTS

108
CANADIAN FOREIGN POLICY AND NATIONAL INTERESTS 1999
James H. Taylor

124
WOMEN IN THE TWENTIETH AND TWENTY-FIRST CENTURIES 1999
Margaret Catley-Carlson

138
SOVEREIGNTY: NOT WHAT IT USED TO BE 1999
Barbara McDougall

148
NINE-ELEVEN AND THE
ISLAMIC FUNDAMENTALIST TERRORIST MINDSET 2002
Peter St. John

160
IRAQ AND THE IMPLICATIONS FOR CANADA 2003
Sir Andrew Burns

168
WORKING WITH AMERICA AFTER 9/11 2004
Colin Robertson

180
A NEW COURT FOR A NEW CENTURY 2005
Lloyd Axworthy

Acknowledgements

I WANT TO ACKNOWLEDGE the assistance of a number of people who allowed this volume to come together so quickly. They include librarian Walter Eisenbeis at the CIIA headquarters in Toronto; Walter supplied crucial material on the early years of the institute, and sent photos and bios of several authors. I am also indebted to Yvonne Rideout of the British High Commission in Ottawa, who suppled the photograph and biography of Sir Andrew Burns; Christina Von Schindler of the University of Winnipeg, who was extremely helpful, not only in supplying Dr. Axworthy's photograph and bio, but also for cheerfully and rapidly preparing his manuscript in printed form.

I also want to thank the authors, Frances Russell, Colin Robertson, Daryl Copeland, Christine Shelly, Si Taylor and Margaret Catley-Carlson, for putting their thoughts formally on paper and kindly forwarding them to me. Thanks are also due to Lloyd Axworthy for allowing us to include his paper in the book.

In Winnipeg, I am indebted to Muriel Smith, Ruth Loutit and Kathleen Burke for both interviews and written materials pertaining to the local branch. And thanks is also due to Dale Walker, the last branch treasurer, who was incredibly helpful in moving the manuscript into reality.

Finally, I am greatly in debt to to Jane Huck, Heather Beattie and Deborah Riley, as well as Barbara Huck and Dawn Huck of Heartland. Jane and Heather spent hours inputting the considerable number of papers that I had acquired over the years; Barbara and Debbie did an excellent job of editing them and made sense of my own blunders of style, while Dawn, as always, turned a jumble of manuscripts into a beautiful book.

Peter St. John
April 2005

Introduction

FROM THE GREAT WAR TO THE GLOBAL VILLAGE: *A Window on the World* combines a history of the Canadian Institute of International Affairs (CIIA) with some of the best papers on Canada's place in the world that have been presented in the past decade.

Though the institute's official launch was in Toronto and its headquarters remains there today, it could fairly be stated that the CIIA really began in Winnipeg. Two of its three early presidents, Edgar Tarr and John W. Dafoe, came from the city, and initially, the Winnipeg branch had the largest membership in Canada. Throughout its seventy-year life, innovation in learning was its watchword.

The CIIA evolved from Dafoe's passionate interest in things international. The long time editor of the *Winnipeg Free Press* was an outspoken, internationally known writer and commentator on foreign affairs and Canada's place in the world. During the late 1930s, his voice, along with that of Winston Churchill, was among the very few who spoke out against accommodating the expansionist tendencies of Adolph Hitler.

Survival on the Canadian Prairies almost necessitates a focus on the outside world and Winnipeggers have made a virtue of international awareness and travel. The city's remarkable multicultural diversity and participation in two world wars have combined to sensitize the community to the wider world. And for seven decades, CIIA members gathered regularly to listen to gifted speakers, form study groups and conduct rigorous debate about global situations from Czechoslovakia to Rwanda and Darfur.

One of those most keenly interested in international affairs was Wilf Queen-Hughes, a journalist with the *Winnipeg Tribune.* Having survived the siege of Hong Kong and spent long years as a POW, Wilf was left with a dual legacy; lifelong bouts of malarial chills and an intense interest in the wider world. When he died, he left a legacy of his own, the Queen-Hughes Bequest. Beginning in 1973 and administered through the Winnipeg Foundation, the fund allowed the CIIA to annually invite distinguished specialists in international affairs to come to Winnipeg to speak at a subsidized dinner. A high point in the year, the Queen-Hughes Lecture was, I believe, unique among all the thirty or more CIIA branches across the country.

The legacy of Wilf Queen-Hughes continues through this volume, for seven chapters in the book are comprised of recent lectures, and the fund contributed to its publication.

By the turn of the twenty-first century, the Winnipeg branch was aging along with some of its most devoted members — among them nonagenarians Reuben Bellan, Gordon MacDonell, and Ruth, Anne and Isobel Loutit. During the 1990s, Ruth and Anne had worked tirelessly to keep the branch alive, encouraging young people to attend and never losing their fascination with things international.

Among the many authors represented here, Colin Robertson probably best epitomizes what the CIIA strives to achieve. Colin became a member while studying at the University of Manitoba and, after graduate work at Carleton University in Ottawa, joined what was then known as the Department of External Affairs. After serving as Canadian Consul in Hong Kong and Los Angeles, he was appointed by the prime minister in 2004 to serve as Canada's Minister (Advocacy) to the United States Congress. The position provides long needed access to Congress for the provinces and Ottawa.

Colin's commitment to the CIIA is evident in his willingness to allow us to include not one, but two of his papers here: his 1997 Queen-Hughes Lecture and a presentation made late in 2004, after he took up his present position. Both greatly contribute to the tone and tenor of the book.

In order to provide necessary context for these and other chapters, I felt it was necessary to give readers some background on the institute. I was aided in this task by Frances Russell, longtime columnist for the *Winnipeg Free Press* and award-winning author, who has always admired the paper's legendary editor and co-founder of the CIIA, John Dafoe.

Frances' opening chapter, 'John W. Dafoe: The *Winnipeg Free Press* and Foreign Policy', tells the tale of the early years of the institute magnificently. I hope my chapter on the next half-century, 'From the Cold War to the New World Order', makes clear the remarkably international focus of even local branches. This idea is greatly enhanced by the chapter that follows, 'The World According to Ottawa', by John Holmes. A diplomat, professor, and CEO of the CIIA for more than a decade, Holmes is at his best here; his chapter should be read by every student of Canadian foreign policy.

The remaining sections are contemporary, based on presentations made between 1997 and 2004. 'Slouching Toward the Millennium', Colin Robertson's 1997 Queen-Hughes Lecture, is an upbeat forecast of future Canadian foreign policy. The 1998 Queen-Hughes Lecture, 'Globalization and the National Prospect' by Daryl Copeland, diplomat and former editor of the CIIA's *Behind the Headlines*, takes a prescient view of globalization.

'The Challenges of Shared Security', by acting U.S. Ambassador Christine Shelly, demonstrates the deft touch of a long time State Department professional. Shelly was on a cross-country tour to meet provincial and territorial leaders when she spoke to the CIIA in 1999. Two years later, though based in the Pentagon, she happened to be out of the country when a plane slammed into her office on September 11th.

In 'Canadian Foreign Policy and National Interests', former undersecretary of state for Foreign Affairs Si Taylor distills decades of wisdom in a paper that was used across Canada in concert with then Foreign Affairs Minister Lloyd Axworthy's public consultations in 1999. The same year, a large international women's conference prefaced the Pan American Games, which were held in Winnipeg, and one of the keynote presentations was Margaret Catley-Carlson's 'Women in the Twentieth and Twenty-first Centuries'. Also in 1999, former Foreign Minister Barbara McDougall, then President and CEO of the CIIA, gave the Queen-Hughes Lecture on eroding state sovereignty following the Cold War. Her remarks are particularly interesting in light of post-2001 developments outlined in later chapters.

'Nine-Eleven and the Islamic Fundamentalist Terrorist Mindset', my 2002 Queen-Hughes Lecture, was taken to CIIA audiences right across Canada. My message: get over the shock of 9/11 and begin to assess the new fundamentalist enemy. British High Commissioner Sir Andrew Burns addressed the U.S.-U.K. response to that enemy in 'Iraq and the Implications for Canada' in 2003. At the time, Canadians were opposed to the invasion of Iraq and his was not a particularly popular message; in retrospect, the ambassador's measured emphasis on the fundamental interests of Canada, the U.K. and the U.S. reads very well indeed.

In 'Working with America after 9/11', Colin Robertson has the penultimate word on the subject. And in 'Court Celebration: the Hope for International Justice in a Post-Iraq World', the Honourable Lloyd Axworthy, who has returned to Manitoba as president of the University of Winnipeg, looks to the future with a discussion of the creation and early development of the International Criminal Court.

So, just as the CIIA itself strives to be, Winnipeg has long been "*A Window on the World*" and *From the Great War to the Global Village* hopes to continue that tradition, combining a profile of a great Manitoban and the history of the institution he inspired, with essays on international relations that attempt, as he did, to educate Canadians about the world in which we live.

Peter St. John
Editor

FRANCES RUSSELL

Frances Russell was born in Winnipeg and graduated in history and political science from the University of Manitoba. A journalist since 1962, she has covered and commented on politics in three provinces and Ottawa, working for *The Winnipeg Tribune*, *United Press International*, *The Globe and Mail*, *The Vancouver Sun* and the *Winnipeg Free Press*.

She is the author of *Mistehay Sakahegan – The Great Lake: The Beauty and The Treachery of Lake Winnipeg*, a best-seller that won the Manitoba Historical Society's Margaret McWilliams Award for Popular History in 2000. Her second book, *The Canadian Crucible: Manitoba's Role in Canada's Great Divide* again won the Manitoba Historical Society's award for Popular History in 2003.

She is married with one son and makes Winnipeg her home.

1928–1945

John W. Dafoe: The Winnipeg Free Press and Foreign Policy

by Frances Russell

Beginnings

> … [W]hat the Free Press thinks today, Western Canada will think tomorrow and the intelligent part of Eastern Canada will think a few years hence.

THOSE PROPHETIC WORDS WERE WRITTEN by historian Frank Underhill, a founder of the League for Social Reconstruction, seven years before the outbreak of the Second World War and a mere three years into what poet W.H. Auden would later describe in his famous poem, 'September 1, 1939', as "a low, dishonest decade".

It was during that decade, the decade of the 1930s, that Canada's most internationally famous and revered newspaper editor, John Wesley Dafoe, stood isolated at home and abroad to write his thundering editorials denouncing appeasement and exhorting his nation and the free world to stand together for collective security against the gathering darkness of Naziism and fascism.

Writing the Foreword for his 1945 book, *The Voice of Dafoe, A Selection of Editorials on Collective Security 1931–1944*, Victor Sifton, then publisher of the *Winnipeg Free Press*, called John Wesley Dafoe "the last of the great editors …"

> During the 1930s, when self-centred nationalism grew rankly throughout the world, and the apostles of appeasement were popular in the land, almost alone he

held steadfast to his faith, and not infrequently incurred the deep displeasure of life-long friends who had succumbed to the temptation of accepting the short-sighted, and as it turned out, the disastrous, policy of no-commitments and splendid isolation.

At the invitation of Prime Minister Sir Robert Borden, Dafoe went to the Paris Peace Conference of 1919 as one of the advisors to the Canadian delegation. The experience changed his life, making him a life-long advocate of strong multilateral institutions to regulate relations among nations and peoples to ensure global peace and prosperity. Nationalism, he said, could no longer be unlimited.

Though he came to know it was doomed, he never departed from publicly supporting the tragically flawed League of Nations. He knew, as the world knows today, that standing alone, we all fall. Only together is the hope of mankind.

That insight was undoubtedly why, nine years later, in 1928, Dafoe was also invited by Borden to attend a meeting at his house to ratify the constitution of the new Canadian Institute of International Affairs (CIIA), an independent body for the study of foreign policy, affiliated with the Institute of Pacific Relations (IPR) and the London-based Royal Institute of International Affairs (RIIA). This collection of active and engaged scholars, businessmen and senior public servants from coast to coast in Canada would go on to provide most of the individual and intellectual capital for the 'golden age' of Canada's External Affairs Department in the immediate post-war world.

The institute reflected all the many shades of opinion of Canada's role in the world animating Canadians themselves. Its membership included imperialists, nationalists and continentalists and was split between collective security and North American isolationism.

Carter Manny, whose 1971 Harvard University thesis on the CIIA remains its most definitive history, says Dafoe was unique in the CIIA because he belonged to each of the three distinct groups comprising its membership: businessmen, academics and a core of 'elder statesmen'. He had been a Canadian representative at the Paris Peace Conference and thus qualified as an elder statesman; he was concerned with business, especially the grain trade, and, though he was not an academic, his views on foreign policy commanded a national audience and therefore were more influential than those of any scholar.

> During his lifetime, he was the institute's most vocal member ... [He] was a leader of the nationalist wing of internationalist thought ... His concern with business and international trade was also incorporated in his internationalism. These elements led to an unswerving faith in the League of Nations. Through the League, [Dafoe believed] Canadian nationalism could be demonstrated through action independent of Britain, peace could be maintained by collective security and international free trade could eventually be realized.

The CIIA remained an integral part of Dafoe's life to its end. He emerged as its most illustrious member. Though he served as its president for only one year and as president of its companion body, the IPR, for a similarly short time, he was always active behind the scenes. Indeed, he probably ensured its survival at crucial points in its sometimes tumultuous history.

The Winnipeg branch — Dafoe's branch — was the largest in the CIIA family. It was also the most community oriented, the only one to engage the wider public in the great issues of the day through an annual series of radio broadcasts. The members, including Dafoe and Edgar J. Tarr, president of the Monarch Life Assurance Company of Winnipeg, were staunch Canadian nationalists, suspicious of British imperialism and especially the British ruling class, admirers of the United States and, above all, internationalists and interventionists. They called themselves 'the Sanhedrin' after the supreme council and highest court of justice at Jerusalem, which dealt with the religious problems of the Jewish world in New Testament times. Their dinner meetings were held at Childs Restaurant in downtown Winnipeg, while their more intimate gatherings occurred in the fourth floor editorial offices of the Old Lady of Carlton Street — the home of Dafoe's newspaper, the *Winnipeg Free Press*.

To the chagrin of today's historians, guest speakers were guaranteed anonymity to ensure total frankness. Thus, the speeches and the after-dinner discussions that followed have been forever lost. But it takes little imagination to assume, given the influence and calibre of the Winnipeg members, that they heard from most, if not all, of the powerful politicians and civil servants of the time. It also takes little imagination to deduce that Dafoe learned, contributed and seeded the information gleaned from these seminars in the powerful prose that daily graced his newspaper's increasingly prestigious editorial page. Perhaps most important of all, Dafoe's membership in the institute helped prompt his ever-widening correspondence on international matters with such individuals as J. Bartlet Brebner, professor of History at Columbia University, J.F. Green of the American Foreign Policy Association in New York, J.T. Shotwell of the Carnegie Endowment for International Peace and Viscount Astor of the RIIA.

As Sifton stated in his foreword to the compendium of the Dafoe's best editorials, editorials that made the *Free Press* one of the great English-speaking newspapers in the world:

> … drawing on a wealth of experience derived from his participation in the periodical conferences of the Canadian Institute for International Affairs … and as Chairman of the Institute for Pacific Relations … [Dafoe] set forth with vigour and clarity his views on the necessity of organized peace. Argument, exhortation, and, if need be, denunciation, were all weapons to be used without fear or favour …

Writing in 1945, a year after Dafoe's death, Sifton had the advantage of hindsight. But Frank Underhill's comment about the power of the editor's thought and writing, published in the October 1932 issue of *Canadian Forum*, took the measure of the man much earlier.

His assessment was validated in Dafoe's most famous editorial, written in 1938 right after Munich, the nadir of collective security. The *Manchester Guardian* still has on its website its picture of British Prime Minister Neville Chamberlain disembarking from his airplane at Heston airport, holding aloft, fluttering in the wind, a piece of paper bearing "Herr Hitler's signature" and claiming he had secured "peace in our time".

Dafoe was then in Ottawa as part of his duties as a member of the Royal Commission on Dominion-Provincial Relations, otherwise known as the Rowell-Sirois commission. Inflamed, he sent the lead editorial back to Winnipeg by wire. Dated September 30, 1938 and headlined 'What's the Cheering For', the editorial is perhaps the most memorable he ever wrote:

> While the cheers are proceeding over the success which is attending the project of dismembering a state by process of bloodless aggression, some facts might be set out for the information of people who would like to know what the cheering is about and who ought to be taking part in it … Nazi aggression … excludes as worthless agreements,

engagements, pledges, guarantees, when they get in the way of desire for aggression and the power to effect it. Austria yesterday, Czechoslovakia today; what of tomorrow and the day after ... The doctrine that Germany can intervene for racial reasons for the 'protection' of Germans on such grounds as she thinks proper in any country in the world which she is in a position to coerce, and without regard to any engagements she has made or guarantees she has given, has now not only been asserted but made good; and it has been approved, sanctioned, certified and validated by the Governments of Great Britain and France, who have undertaken in this respect to speak for the democracies of the world ... This is the situation; and those who think it is all right will cheer for it.

In his biography of the great editor, University of Manitoba political scientist Murray Donnelly wrote that the *Free Press* was one of the few newspapers in the world to see the Munich settlement for what it was. *The Times* of London, under the editorship of Geoffrey Dawson, was one of the worst apologists for Chamberlain's appeasement. "No conqueror returning from a victory on the battlefield has come home adorned with nobler laurels than Mr. Chamberlain from Munich," it said and continued, "... [T]here is no doubt that Mr. Chamberlain offered concession from strength and not from weakness."

The Manchester Guardian was no better. "... [G]reat as are the injustices that Czechosolovakia suffers under the Munich agreement, and they are for her calamitous, they cannot be measured against the horrors that might have extinguished not only Czechosolovakia, but the whole of western civilization."

Many Canadian newspapers had been sounding a similarly craven note for years. When Hitler entered the Rhineland in March 1936, *The Vancouver Sun* opined: "Canadians who do not allow themselves to be swayed by a personal dislike for Hitler and his unpleasant colleagues will feel a measure of sympathy for this new attitude of the German people ... Canada is only a spectator. There are not enough moral principles at stake to induce her to become otherwise."

Penned *The Edmonton Bulletin*: "After eighteen years, Europe can afford to restore Germany to full standing in the concert of nations." Agreed *The Montreal Gazette*: "Nothing can ever be gained by persistently treating

Germany as though she was national enemy No.1 in perpetuity. It would likewise be dangerous and futile to regard Adoph Hitler in no other light than as one whose designs are willfully antagonistic to forces that hate war."

Dafoe's passionate support of the League of Nations and its promise of collective security was one of only two occasions in his forty-three-year stewardship of the *Free Press* (continuously from 1901 until his death in 1944) that he found himself at odds with his political home, the Liberal Party of Canada, and the two prime ministers he knew intimately, Sir Wilfrid Laurier and William Lyon Mackenzie King.

The first split occurred when Laurier, in opposition and fearful of losing Québec to Henri Bourassa's nationalists, refused to join Robert Borden's Union government during the First World War. Dafoe, even then seeing Canada "as part of a wider world in which it had international interests and responsibilities," rallied western Liberals to Borden's side and openly campaigned against Laurier in the 1917 election.

The break was thus made irreparable between the editor and the former prime minister. Writing in *Scrum Wars,* historian Allan Levine says that, angered at losing Dafoe's support and concerned the editor had grown too powerful for his own good, Laurier considered starting his own morning paper in Winnipeg in 1918, a year before he died.

It was left to Laurier's heir, King, to bring Dafoe back on side. King offered Dafoe a House of Commons seat in the election of 1926, but Dafoe declined, telling him he would "sooner be the editor of the *Free Press* than the Prime Minister of Canada." Following the Liberal victory in 1935 — a victory clearly assisted by the *Free Press'* relentless attacks on incumbent Tory Prime Minister R.B. Bennett whom Dafoe despised — King gave him his choice of a cabinet post or the Washington ambassadorship. Again, Dafoe turned him down. This relative closeness meant an open and hostile rift like that with Laurier never happened between Dafoe and King. Another reason may have been the fact Dafoe's work on the royal commission kept him off his editorial page for much of the two years prior to the outbreak of war in 1939.

While it would be too strong to say the appeasement newspapers spoke for the King government, the prime minister viewed all Canada's foreign relations through the prism of domestic policy. For him, the unity of Canada trumped all else. Simply, he would not risk it, perhaps following the dictum of an unknown MP in 1923 who said simply: "Let us … conciliate Québec and Ontario before we start conciliating Roumania and Ukrainia."

The prime minister had an intuitive connection with his fractured land and always remained equivocal until the moment decision could not be postponed further. Because his obscurantism reflected the ambivalence in the public itself, King's purposeful dithering seemed to help him prod Canadians along to accept his decisions when they were finally made.

"King could not be budged," writes Manny. "The success of his policy in keeping a divided country together demonstrated that Canada could commit herself only if that commitment did not threaten internal unity. Unlike most countries, Canada could not go to war abroad without risking immediate civil war at home. King's policy centred on minimizing this risk."

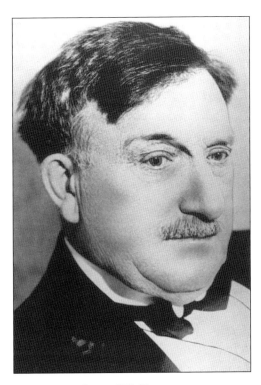

JOHN W. DAFOE

Thus, as Manny and others have observed, not all of Dafoe's impassioned editorials taken together, nor the CIIA, which itself split on the issue of interventionism and non-interventionism as the war drums beat louder, could have affected foreign policy. The prime minister kept the country united, and, in the end, was able to take it to war a mere week after Britain's declaration, by sticking to his pledge that "Parliament (that is, Canada alone) will decide."

Both King and Dafoe had to tack against an isolationist tide in Canada almost as strong as that pulling the United States. As a newspaper editor, Dafoe feared no immediate consequences. King, however, had his country to consider.

An esteemed Liberal and Laurier's minister of the interior, Clifford Sifton, had been Dafoe's first publisher and was the father of his second, Victor. He made no secret of his isolationist bent in this communication with Dafoe in 1920: "The League of Nations is a preposterous and expensive farce and amounts to nothing more than a part of a machine designed to involve us in European and Imperialistic complications. Canada ought to call a halt to this business."

The relationship between Dafoe and King must have been incredibly complex. A son of Orange Ontario, Dafoe reflected its anti-French Canadian, anti-Roman Catholic prejudices his entire life. He refused to accept that Canada was a bilingual country. He agreed with the abolition of the official status of the French language and confessional schools in Manitoba in 1890. And he viewed the Cathedral in St. Boniface as an outpost of French Canadian control from Québec. As prime minister, King could not afford the luxury of not understanding fully thirty per cent of Canada and the root and branch of his party's support.

In 1943, a year before his death, the editor himself attempted to codify his own feelings about his long relationship with Canada's strangest, but in political terms, most successful, prime minister: "My relations with King have never got to the point of warm friendship, but they have been close enough to give me an impression … that there is more to this man than I have thought."

King met Hitler in 1937 following the Imperial Conference. He immediately illustrated his legendary ambiguity. He said to Hitler's face in Berlin that in the event of "a war of aggression, nothing in the world would keep the Canadian people from being at the side of Britain." But immediately upon his return to Canada, he told journalist Bruce Hutchinson that Hitler was "a simple sort of peasant, not very intelligent and no serious danger to anyone … obsessed with the recovery of neighbouring territory inhabited by Germans, a natural feeling. When he had brought these territories into the Reich … he would be satisfied … he would not risk a large war."

While King, unlike Laurier, never had to face the redoubtable editor in open electoral battle, Dafoe still stung him with his pen, again for his uncertain support of the League and collective security. One editorial, headlined 'Mr. King at Geneva', published October 1, 1936, sternly criticized King for trying to have it both ways. King, Dafoe wrote, wanted to keep Canada's membership in the League while insisting that it and other member nations had the right to follow or ignore its covenant at will. Warning that such a policy would turn the League into "the most pitiable and transparent humbug of all time," Dafoe continued:

> This is the last in a long series of acts by successive Canadian governments intended to circumscribe the League's powers; and it is the most discreditable of them all because it amounts to a rejection by Canada of the League … These propositions are unworthy of Mr. King and if

adopted as governing principles of policy would be discreditable to Canada, and, in the long run, ruinous to the peace and prosperity of this country.

Yet, as Levine writes, as early as 1936, Dafoe was already privately conceding that the League was "doomed and King could not have saved the institution". When King learned of this, he became understandably irritated at Dafoe's occasional chiding. This, Levine continues, apparently pleased Dafoe, who, who despite his devotion to Liberalism, believed that "the newspaper whose support of a party is bought and paid for directly or indirectly out of party funds, is a propagandist sheet and not a public journal."

When war came, however, Dafoe rallied to the prime minister, accepting, albeit reluctantly, the government's rejection both of conscription and coalition.

Covering all eventualities as usual, King paid a quiet visit to Winnipeg in the early summer of 1941 to ensure this powerful editor's support. There, in the fourth floor editorial offices at 300 Carlton Street, he met with Dafoe and his managing editor, George Ferguson.

Dafoe told the prime minister flatly he would not support him if his government opposed conscription on principle. King pledged to "tackle it". Dafoe reluctantly agreed to the ingenious 'out' the prime minister had devised to solve his political predicament in French Canada — a plebiscite asking Canadians to release the government from its anti-conscription pledge. Nevertheless, Dafoe condemned it as "an unheroic expedient to protect the country against the dangers and consequences of ill-considered courses urged by reckless men."

Afterwards, showing a bit of the ambiguity of King himself, Dafoe admitted — privately only — that his respect for the prime minister had soared. He told a friend in 1942 that "King is about as indispensable for Canada as Roosevelt is for the United States or Churchill for Great Britain."

Certainly, King was never to experience the opprobrium Dafoe heaped upon Britain's traitorous Cliveden Set. It reached its zenith in the March 10, 1938 editorial headlined 'The League Won't Work … Of Course Not! And Why?' Furious that, according to Lord Beaverbrook, Lord Astor and his pro-Nazi upper-class friends had called the League of Nations an anti-German military bloc, Dafoe came out with all guns blazing:

> Lord Astor … is one of the 'authoritarian group' who decide what the foreign policy of Great Britain is. It

naturally follows that they will see to it that Great Britain will give no support to the League now that it has descended to the level of an 'anti-German bloc', which, even in its decrepit state, might still offer resistance to the destruction of Czechoslovakia and the over-running of the Danubian and Balkan countries.

The plans formulated two years ago by what has come to be known (and which will have its own black page in history) as the 'Cliveden Set' have thus been carried to a triumphant conclusion. They are now the proclaimed policies of Great Britain; and so far as the Government of that country is concerned, the way is now clear for the Nazi legions to move for the building up of that huge Fascist fortress in Middle Europe so ardently desired by … the 'Cliveden Set'.

Dafoe found himself isolated on yet another baleful attribute of the 1930s and beyond, the scourge of anti-Semitism. He used his pen on several occasions to flay its apostles, though he ignored the Liberal government's "none is too many" immigration policy regarding European Jews attempting to flee Nazi persecution.

Hitler's ascension to the chancellorship of Germany on January 30, 1933, caused Dafoe, in biographer Donnelly's words, "to see the international situation in the blackest terms" and to begin to predict the inevitability of what he would come to call the "hyperbolic war". In March of that year, Dafoe wrote a series of editorials expressing his foreboding. "A wild patriot has been thrown into power in Germany on a wave of desperation and hope … [S]hould Germany and Italy come together, France will be faced with a dilemma and what will happen to Poland?" he asked on March 20th.

Then, a few days later, came this, sounding the alarms for the first time about the rise of anti-Semitism in Germany: "There is no mania quite so self-revealing as that of Jew-baiting … The nation that indulges in it 'places' and 'dates' itself far beyond the power of the most skillful casuist to enter apology or defence."

Throughout this tumultuous period, Dafoe was beset with many troubles revolving around his 'child', the CIIA. Although the organization was not founded until 1928, its origins began with the Paris Peace Conference of 1919. British and American delegates were concerned about widespread public apathy and ignorance of international affairs that conceivably might lead to yet another conflict down the road. The RIIA was founded in London in 1920 and among the original members were ten Canadians. By 1926, there were about twenty-six RIIA members in Canada, many of whom were also members of the League of Nations Society formed in 1921. Meanwhile, in the United States, the returning Americans discovered that the Council on Foreign Relations had already been formed, so they joined it rather than creating another institute.

In 1925, a delegation of six Canadians headed by John Nelson, *Macleans'* magazine's Vancouver correspondent and an ardent Rotarian who later became the public relations supervisor for the Sun Life Assurance Company of Montreal, attended a conference in Honolulu at which the Institute for Pacific Relations (IPR) was founded. The Canadians realized they would have to create a new organization to ensure Canada's voice was heard at future IPR conferences. Nelson sparked the formation of IPR branches in Vancouver, Montréal and Toronto, which quickly attracted those Canadian members of the RIIA.

In the fall of 1926, Canadians interested in the RIIA and the IPR met in Toronto to create a new Canadian organization affiliated with both. The next year, the RIIA agreed to accept affiliation with the Toronto group, which became the first branch of the future Canadian Institute of International Affairs. By the end of that year, branches were set up in Montréal and Vancouver. Following the 1927 meeting of the IPR, other branches were established in Ottawa and Winnipeg. The Winnipeg branch absorbed three local groups which had established the Canadian League in 1925. The Winnipeg branch was the largest of the original branches and one of the most active during the Thirties.

As previously noted, the CIIA was formally created at a meeting at former prime minister Borden's Ottawa home in 1928 and committed to affiliation with both the IPR and the RIIA. The founding members came from all five branches: Borden and C.A. Bowman from Ottawa; Sir Arthur Currie, John Nelson and Frederick N. Southam from Montréal; Sir Joseph Flavelle, Newton W. Rowell, Charles S. MacInnes and N.A.M. MacKenzie from Toronto; Dafoe and John MacKay from Winnipeg, and Reginald Brock and Stanley Brent from Vancouver.

Following in the footsteps of the RIIA, the CIIA adopted two fundamental bylaws. "Firstly, that the Institute should not offer any opinion on the conduct of public policy and secondly, that its membership should be confined to British subjects." (There was no Canadian citizenship at that time.) This restriction was subsequently dropped.

The CIIA grew quickly, both in numbers and locations. In 1927, there were thirty-two members of the RIIA in Canada. By the next year, the five original branches totalled 144 members. In 1929, a branch was formed in Regina, in 1931 in Edmonton and Halifax, in 1932 in Saskatoon and Calgary, in 1933 in Hamilton and Kingston, in 1934 in Fredericton and Windsor, in 1936 in Victoria and Saint John and in 1937 in London. Since then there have been branches in Québec City (1943), Sherbrooke-Lennoxville (1944), Camp Borden (1947), Kitchener-Waterloo (1947), St. John's (1949), New York (1963), Wolfville (1964), Sackville (1966), Saguenay (1966), West Kootenay (1966), Niagara Region (1974) and Thunder Bay (1981). In the 1970s, French-speaking branches were founded in Montréal, Sept-Iles, Québec City and Moncton. Women's branches were formed in Ottawa, Toronto, London, Winnipeg, Saskatoon and Vancouver, but later amalgamated with the men's branches.

From 1928 to 1932, the branches were the centre of institute activity. The central organization, the Executive Council, formed of two members from each branch, met only once a year during this period. Until 1931, the institute's most important position, that of secretary, was filled on a part-time basis by Nelson. Lacking any full-time staff or officers, the central office was very weak.

The institute's membership drew from two very distinct and, in some cases opposed, worlds — business and academe. As earlier pointed out, Carter Manny also identified a third, very small but influential group of prestigious 'elder statesmen', whose preeminence in the realm of government and public affairs accorded them special importance in the institute's activities and helped it attract new members of high calibre. The businessmen dominated the organizational positions and were active in arranging and participating in branch meetings, while the academics dominated the institute's research work, primarily preparing papers for the IPR conferences. Indeed, the IPR, rather than its own affairs, appeared to be the main reason for the CIIA's existence in the early years.

The institute's 'town and gown' division began to cause problems almost immediately. This was the golden age of exclusive gentlemen's clubs and the CIIA quickly emerged as an ideal vehicle for wealthy businessmen and men of leisure to make influential international contacts in Britain and elsewhere. Writes Manny: "The CIIA was an elitist group and it became rather a matter of prestige to belong to it. Joining the CIIA was like joining a good club, and this attitude did not lead to the soundest intellectual activity or interest."

As early as 1931, Edgar Tarr, then a Winnipeg lawyer and one of the institute's most active presidents, wanted to get rid of some of this "dead wood", but his desires were never acted upon. Manny speculates this 'dead wood' may have contributed to the lack of enthusiasm among academics for the institute's work in its early years.

In January 1932, at the institute's fifth annual meeting, the central organization began a new, more assertive role assisted by a five-year, $21,000 grant from the Massey Foundation to hire a full-time national secretary. A search was commenced and Dafoe suggested Escott Reid, son of an Anglican clergyman from Campbellford in Ontario's Trent Valley, a bright young intellectual and Rhodes Scholar. In June, the executive unanimously accepted Dafoe's recommendation and elected Reid. The energetic and idealistic future foreign affairs bureaucrat immediately began to revolutionize the institute.

In his 1989 autobiography, *Radical Mandarin: The Memoirs of Escott Reid*, Reid looked back on that time and provided an illuminating description of the institute's internal schism.

> The Canadian Institute of International Affairs had a divided personality. The dominant group at its foundation in 1928 were the Canadian members of the Royal Institute of International Affairs ... Some were elder statesmen like Sir Robert Borden, Newton Rowell and Sir Arthur Currie; others, like Vincent Massey, were public-spirited, well-to-do, and influential in public affairs. This group was, in the terminology of the time, imperialist — that is, they believed in close links between Canada and Britain and a closely knit empire. Another group came into the CIIA through the Institute of Pacific Relations, when the institute became the Canadian unit of the IPR. This group was on the whole younger and included more academics, most of whom did not believe in close links between Canada and Britain or a closely knit empire ... Of course not all the early members of the CIIA could be fitted into one of these three compartments. J.W. Dafoe, editor of the *Winnipeg Free Press* and the leading newspaper editor of his time, was an internationalist, a nationalist, and no great admirer of the British governing classes or of the British Empire. Edgar Tarr of Winnipeg held much the same views as Dafoe. Rowell, in a letter in October 1933, said of Tarr, 'We do not see eye to eye on Empire problems.'

As national secretary, Reid believed in the value of conferences to motivate members and co-ordinate research. In the fall of 1933, he proposed that the CIIA hold the first of what he hoped would be regular national study conferences. It occurred in May 1934. Writes Manny:

> Reid's centralizing efforts had occupational and ideological overtones. Businessmen had neither the time nor the desire, in most cases, to do research work. An increased emphasis on research work meant an increase in the importance of the institute's academic members. Many of these academics were young intellectuals, who, like Reid, held 'left wing' views … If the institute became predominantly a research organization the businessmen would probably leave. They were unwilling or unable to participate in research and were ideologically incompatible with the young left wing intellectuals.

The ideological tension began to build. The young intellectuals opposed uncontrolled international trade, believing it bred inequality among nations, while the businessmen thought the freer the trade the better it was for business and nations alike.

Rowell, a CIIA founder, was a distinguished Canadian with an illustrious career that included a portfolio in Borden's wartime cabinet, the post of chief justice of Ontario and the position of commissioner in the landmark investigation of federal-provincial fiscal relations that colloquially bears his name. He was one of the first members to take umbrage at Reid's views and activities, resigning as the institute's president in 1933. In a letter to Dafoe, Rowell said the institute should not become "a kind of university extension course in international affairs … If branches do not wish to take up the serious study of any particular question or questions, they must be perfectly free to do so without question or criticism …" In his reply, Dafoe indicated he shared Rowell's view, but he stopped short of criticizing his protégé, Reid.

Businessmen supplied the institute with most of its funds and also helped to keep the institute true to its constitutionally-mandated neutrality by balancing the left wing opinions of the young intellectuals and academics. Rowell's complaints to Dafoe were prophetic. In 1934, the institute experienced a financial crisis, in part because of growing dissatisfaction with the political leanings and centralizing ambitions of its national secretary.

In the winter of 1934–35, the Winnipeg Branch sponsored a series of twenty-six radio broadcasts, the first use of radio by the institute. States Manny: "That these weekly broadcasts were sponsored by the businessmen-dominated Winnipeg branch … may indicate a more realistic attitude toward the education of the public on the part of the CIIA businessmen members." The Winnipeg branch also later established a liaison with the World Affairs Council of Minneapolis characterized by regular exchanges.

The CIIA passed an important milestone in the spring of 1935 when it became officially bilingual as L'Institute Canadien des Affaires Internationales. During the early 1930s, there had been very few French Canadian members and only two could be described as active. This led Manny to compare the status of French Canadians in the CIIA to the status of black Americans in most U.S. corporations until quite recently. A few 'tokens' were included "to show the absence of discrimination".

During this same period, a clash of identity as old as Canada itself reappeared in the institute. It was not new, having marked the institute's founding. Many Canadian nationalists wanted no part of the early efforts to open Canadian chapters of the RIIA, fearing it would cement Canada's colonial status and deny it its opportunity to develop its own identity and foreign policy. Now, a decade later, the struggle was re-engaged on another front. 'Collectivists' wanted Canada's foreign policy to be dominated by its obligations to the League of Nations, while 'traditionalists' wanted Canadian policy to follow in lock-step with Britain. A third group, 'non-interventionists', like their counterparts in the United States, wanted to keep Canada out of all wars.

This ideological tug-of-war was further complicated by the left-right divisions within the institute. Among the collectivists, the left believed in what it called "peace with justice", that is, that sanctions should not be used against an aggressor unless the League also attempted to solve the aggressor's economic problems. The right-wing or 'hard line' collectivists wanted sanctions to be enforced unconditionally.

Italy's invasion of Ethiopia in September 1935 was a turning point in Canadian internationalist thought. The Liberal government's adoption of economic sanctions against Italy was attacked by the peace with justice collectivists. But when that same government repudiated its representative to the League, W. A. Riddell, for proposing that oil be included on the list of sanctions, it was the hardliners' turn to be angry. When Addis Ababa fell in June 1936 and it became clear sanctions had not worked and the League had not stopped aggression, the institute — and Canadians generally — split into two camps: those who favoured Canadian participation in the next 'Great War' and those who wanted neutrality.

The Ethiopian question drove another wedge between Dafoe and Reid. Dafoe was a hard-line collectivist while Reid was a charter member of the peace with justice collectivists. They clashed openly at a meeting of the National Council of the League of Nations Society (LNS) in November 1935. (Not surprisingly, there was a huge overlap in the memberships of the CIIA and the LNS.)

Reid presented a motion calling for the Canadian government to pursue a collective effort with other nations to achieve a peaceful solution to the world's "… territorial, economic and population problems" and to refuse to continue sanctions against Italy and withdraw from the league unless other league members worked towards this solution.

Rowell and Dafoe spoke out against Reid and succeeded in defeating his motion. Nevertheless, Dafoe appeared to moderate his hard line later after Justice Minister Ernest Lapointe censured Riddell. Perhaps because of his overall support for the King Liberals, Dafoe contented himself with merely labelling as "unfortunate" Lapointe's repudiation of Canada's emissary to the League of Nations.

Throughout the fall of 1935 and the spring of 1936, Escott Reid continued to argue his case before the court of public opinion in a series of articles in *Canadian Forum* and other organs. This outspokenness made him the institute's most controversial figure. By the spring of 1936, Reid had moved from peace with justice to outright non-intervention, arguing that Canada was not bound by the League and therefore could drop sanctions against Italy. Says Manny: "His arguments were not so much for 'peace with justice' as they were against Canadian involvement in the next 'Great War.'"

As the controversy swirled around its outspoken national secretary, some of the institute's most influential members began to contemplate his removal. In a letter dated January 10, 1936, Rowell noted Reid's term was to expire the next August and proposed his reappointment be discussed at the meeting of the CIIA National Council in February. The former war council chairman in Borden's cabinet stated baldly that "we [the council and Reid] should come to some understanding about propaganda." In his reply to Rowell, Dafoe tried to pour oil on troubled waters. While he shared Rowell's sentiments, he warned it would be unwise for the institute to interfere with Reid's freedom of speech. He thought the best solution would be for the council to convince Reid to be more discreet. The editor carefully avoided advocating Reid's dismissal, fearing a war of personalities might erupt, break out into the open and discredit the institute. It was becoming obvious, however, that Reid's forthright views were a divisive force that only served to increase the ideological tensions within the institute.

In reality, the institute was merely a reflection of the country and Canadian public opinion in turn a reflection of the tumult of that "low, dishonest decade". Manny writes: "As the world drifted towards war, debate over Canada's foreign policy became a debate over war and peace. Canadian internationalists and the Canadian public in general were becoming divided into two groups: interventionists and non-interventionists.

Reid continued on his activist, centralist course throughout the rest of 1936, touring the branches and proposing the institute use its resources to inform the public on international affairs. At one point, he even suggested members send in their papers from the various conferences they had attended so they could be distributed by the institute to the nation's libraries. He wanted the branches to follow detailed study outlines prepared by the national headquarters and to hold regular meetings.

Reid's 'five year plan', circulated to the membership in January 1937, stressed educating the public. He recommended that potential leaders of public opinion, such as journalists, teachers and MPs, be elected to the institute, that the institute encourage and assist the writing and publication of books and articles, that it cooperate with other organizations to promote itself and its publications and that it sponsor radio broadcasts and provide information to newspapers. He wanted to increase the institute's membership among heretofore under-represented minorities, including women, French Canadians and Canadians of non-British, non-French background.

Once again, Reid put himself on a confrontation course with his employers, particularly the institute's founders and wealthy business contributors. His proposals for public education activities threatened the institute's founding 'no policy' rule. And his idea to make the institute more representative of Canadian society threatened the institute's atmosphere as an exclusive gentlemen's club, something certain to cost it both membership and money. Finally, increased recruitment of French and other European Canadians would strengthen the institute's non-interventionist wing, further alienating the business group who tended to support Canadian belligerence.

Dafoe was CIIA president at the time of Reid's mailing. It alarmed him. In a letter to E.C. Carter, an official of the American IPR, the editor was highly critical.

> The situation created by Mr. Reid's letter to the council … has reached a point where it will have to be dealt with. As you know, I thought this letter both injudicious in its timing and its contents … If we can see our way to the necessary funds Mr. Reid's ambitious programme may be adopted in some form or other. Failing this, we shall have perhaps to reduce our activities, in which case there is the possibility, I fancy, that Mr. Reid may decide to retire.

Former CIIA president Vincent Massey, who much later was to serve as Canada's first Canadian governor general, went further. He announced in a letter to Dafoe that his family's foundation was not going to renew its grant to the institute, the grant that had been paying Reid's salary as national secretary since 1933. Wrote Massey:

> I cannot help feeling that there is some doubt as to the wisdom of embarking on the programme of development which has recently been under consideration … there are, I feel, definite disadvantages in building up too much machinery at headquarters and emphasizing out of its relative position those various activities which come under the heading of Research.

Reid took a leave of absence from the institute in the fall of 1937, at the same time that Tarr replaced Dafoe as president. Reid's job was assumed on a temporary basis by E.B. Rogers, whom Manny describes as a "moderate" like the new president. Tarr went about soothing bruised feelings by touring the branches and stressing that members' suggestions were again welcome at national headquarters. He wanted inspiration to flow from the branches to the centre rather than the other way around as Reid's centralism had attempted. While the institute's existing public education functions continued, plans for ambitious reforms were abandoned. "Tarr had the time, energy and intellectual capacity to assert ideologically moderate leadership and was instrumental in healing the division which threatened the institute," writes Manny.

Reid returned briefly in July 1938, but submitted his resignation later that month to take effect October 31, 1938. In 1939, he became second secretary of the Canadian Legation in Washington, D.C. Just prior to his resignation, he prepared another memorandum outlining his ambitions for the CIIA. His youthful idealism fairly shone off every page. He wanted the institute to be an accurate reflection of Canadian society, encourage controversy as well as objectivity and assert more active leadership of public opinion. He wrote:

> I have been possessed … with the idea that it is possible for the Canadian Institute of International Affairs to lay within the next decade the foundations in Canada of a democracy which will have a sufficiently accurate knowledge and a significantly wise understanding of international affairs to be able to conduct its external relations on a higher plane than any nation has yet reached.

In his memoirs Reid made it clear he bore no grudge against Dafoe and Tarr, saying "My three heroes of the thirties were Frank Underhill, Edgar Tarr and J.W. Dafoe." But as noted earlier, he made no secret of his opposition to Massey and Rowell.

> Rowell and Massey were devoted admirers of the British and of the Royal Institute for International Affairs … [Massey] wanted to have Royal added to [the CIIA's] name. I did nothing about this and this may have rankled … Perhaps the reason Rowell and Massey were opposed to the institute establishing study groups, holding conferences, and publishing books was that they had discovered at the British Commonwealth Relations Conference in 1933 that younger Canadians, particularly younger academics, did not share their devotion to the British Empire and their trust in the wisdom and good faith of National or Conservative governments in Britain.

Reid went on to note that Massey

> … had doubts about many of the people that were members of the institute — at least of its Montréal branch … [writing] in his diary that it was 'a rather frigid, over-intellectual body dominated by able but rather arrogant young men.' It may be that the arrogant young men had been unresponsive to his talk on Canadian foreign policy

because they were reluctant to express openly their opposition to his views ... As long as the institute held only confidential branch meetings addressed by visitors, the dissident views of the younger members had limited opportunities for expression. Once the institute started study groups and held national study conferences and published books on Canadian foreign policy, the dissidents would have ample opportunity to air their views and make converts. This is indeed what happened.

Reid also reflected, perhaps a bit ruefully, on himself. "Excess of zeal exacerbated by an addiction to working too hard has too often led me, before and after joining External Affairs, to being impatient and provocative on issues I have felt deeply about."

After Reid's departure, John R. Baldwin became the institute's new national secretary. While what Manny calls "the divisive movement towards a centralized, academic-dominated organization ended," the institute did establish publications and public education committees, launched a campaign to enlist newspapers as corporate subscribers in return for which they would receive CIIA publications and other information on international affairs and began to publish books.

Included among the titles were *The Canadian Economy and Its Problems*, edited by H.A. Innis and A.F.W. Plumptre; *Canada Looks Abroad*, by R.A. MacKay and E.B. Rogers, and *Canada and the Pacific and War*, by William Strange. *Canada Today*, by F.R. Scott, a survey of Canadian internationalist opinion prepared for the 1938 British Commonwealth Relations Conference, was the most successful of the institute's early books. Published in 1939, it went to a second edition, in which Scott concluded that Canada would make an economic, if not a military, contribution to the coming war and also participate in any pan-American defence system. As continuing evidence of the sharp ideological splits within the membership, first drafts of Scott's work circulated to many leading CIIA members prompted grumblings that his socialist ideas should be subdued.

As the war drums beat louder, the institute roiled with its own internal conflict between non-interventionists and supporters of collective security. By now, the cleavage was clearly along left-right lines. Those, such as Edgar MacInnes and Frank Underhill, who had participated in founding the left-leaning League for Social Reconstruction, advocated non-intervention. MacInnes opposed Canadian belligerence, arguing that Canada would be fighting for Britain, not democracy. He accused the Liberal government of keeping Canadians ignorant so it could drag the country into war. Underhill echoed MacInnes' criticism of the government and went even further in criticizing the interventionists. He claimed that all with the exception of Dafoe had revealed "… themselves as only British imperialists in disguise."

For his part, Dafoe was as vigorous as ever in his support for collective security. He attacked those who wanted to "reform" the League, charging that their socialist proposals would destroy it. While Dafoe endorsed a Commonwealth alliance as one way to establish a collective system, Scott denounced it, claiming the Commonwealth was an artificial creation which could never provide the security of a truly "world society". By "world society", Scott of course meant a socialist society. He also retained fears that Britain controlled Canadian action because its Great Seal was still required for the ratification of Canadian treaties. He proposed Canada take constitutional steps to allow it to proclaim neutrality if Britain went to war. When Cooperative Commonwealth Federation (CCF) leader J.S. Woodsworth presented a neutrality bill to Parliament in January 1937, Dafoe opposed it but continued to back both the government's defence preparations and 'no commitments' foreign policy.

By 1938, Manny says, Dafoe stood alone as the only CIIA member, and the only prominent Canadian, to support the League of Nations. "During the year, he attacked anyone who violated the principles of the League." After Chamberlain made his fateful pact with Hitler in Munich, Dafoe argued that Canada should now turn towards the United States. The editor had long believed that the League would have been successful if the Americans had joined.

While the *Free Press* continued to attack imperialists, socialists and 'realists' for the roles they had played in destroying the League, in a December 30, 1938 editorial, it still urged the government to demonstrate Canada's right to neutrality. The newspaper didn't want Canada to adopt neutrality, but wanted its neutrality clearly asserted so that parliament would be seen to be truly free in deciding whether or not to declare war.

Throughout 1938 and the first eight months of 1939, the public debate between some of the most well-known members of the CIIA became ever more emotional. Scott continued to denounce the 'fight for democracy' argument for belligerence as nothing more than an imperialist hoax. For his part, historian Arthur Lower said Canada would still have to trade with Europe even if the latter fell to fascism. He implied Canada had little to fear from a Europe under Hitler's heel and could defend itself, even without the assistance of the United States. The *Free Press* called Scott "... perhaps the most brilliant English-speaking exponent of isolationism in Canada today," in a July 18, 1938 editorial.

Enraged, Scott began a war of words with the paper that the *Free Press* eagerly joined. Scott cited his membership in the League of Nations Society to insist he wasn't an isolationist. He attacked Canadian imperialists, calling them the real isolationists and citing their lukewarm support of the League and their neutrality over Manchuria and the Spanish Civil War. "[T]he only time the imperialists are not isolationist is when England has decided she cannot remain neutral," he wrote.

In an editorial accompanying Scott's letter, the *Free Press* said he "... can be properly considered a mouthpiece of the only isolationists who, at this moment, have any importance whatever." Manny states that this was the only occasion when the paper even approached direct editorial criticism of a CIIA member.

Even though we know Dafoe had long before concluded the League of Nations was doomed, as late as the end of August, the paper was still expressing the hope that the proposed British, French and Russian "peace front" could halt aggression and be the first step in rebuilding the League.

On September 1, 1939, when Hitler's army marched into Poland, the *Free Press* launched a passionate campaign to arouse support for war. On September 4th, the day after Britain declared war on Germany, the *Free Press* wrote: "Whatever the technical constitutional situation may be until Parliament meets on Thursday [September 7th] the fact is that Canada is at war." That war, the editorial continued, "... is to be a struggle for the individual liberty of every citizen of Canada, for the existence of Canada as a nation and for the preservation of world civilization." On September 10, 1939, the Canadian Parliament and government declared war on Germany, exactly one week after Britain.

In the darkest hours of the war, during the autumn of 1940, the Canadian Broadcasting Corporation invited John W. Dafoe to take part in its series entitled, 'Let's Face the Facts'. Although it never appeared in his paper, it is perhaps the penultimate expression of Dafoe's resolve and character.

As his biographer Donnelly put it, he saw the war as a crusade against the forces of darkness, a crusade that had only one end, victory for the forces of light. He compared Hitler to Alaric the Goth, who sacked Rome, Attila the Hun who spread ruin over Central Europe, Tamerlane, who destroyed much of Arab civilization, and Genghis Khan.

Calling Hitler and his henchmen those "bloody-minded and perverted men," he insisted they could never succeed.

> They cannot afford to leave the light of human freedom shining anywhere in the world … therefore, they wage war, world-wide in its purpose, and by a law of iron necessity this war must go on until it destroys every vestige of freedom in the world, or the dictatorships are themselves consumed in the fires which they have ignited.

Civilization, he agreed, was trembling at the abyss of darkness, slavery, racism and totalitarianism. But he had hope. The courage of the British people demonstrated that humanity's yearning for liberty would triumph. Indeed, as Donnelly says, "he spoke of the crucial period in the past tense". Dafoe went on to say:

> The nearer they [the British] were to disaster the firmer their resolution to resist, the greater their scorn for those who looked to them to yield, the stronger their confidence in their power to meet, to break, and to turn aside the impending fury of the barbarians. That superb courage found expression in the immortal words of Churchill; and as those ringing accents went around the world, the defences of civilization, both moral and material, began everywhere to gather strength.

By then seventy-four, he still had, as Donnelly notes, the energy and stamina to urge the Anglo-Saxon democracies to fight on to prevent a return to the dark ages and create "a world of peaceful cooperation in good work by free men and free nations; a world from which the devil-worship of Mars will be forever outlawed."

In 1943, one year before his death, he had a message that has even greater import today than it did then. Writing to Leighton McCarthy, head of the Canadian legation in Washington, he wanted to ensure that Canada's diplomats in the American capital were keeping their eyes open to any incidents in the making of high policy that ignored Canada or relegated it to its former role as an appendage of Britain and the Empire.

> Canada, without being unnecessarily aggressive in her national attitude, should, whenever the need arises, make it plain to all interested parties that she is the sole judge of what she shall do and how it shall be done, with regard to what she produces and how it is to be distributed, and as well with respect to all other matters which naturally fall within the jurisdiction of an independent nation …

He concluded with what could very well be the epitaph for his long and remarkable life: "We cannot act like a colony of either Great Britain or the United States."

Dafoe, who had lived through Riel's execution, the fateful decision by the Manitoba government in 1890 to abolish the official status of the French language in that province, the Union government and the military service question of 1917, was hard at work and writing ever more eloquently until the day he died, Saturday, January 9, 1944. As the *Free Press's* famous Ottawa correspondent, Grant Dexter, wrote soon after: "At noon last Saturday the chief waved goodbye. He was going home. The work for the weekend had been put in his briefcase. The job for Monday was stacked at one side of his writing table."

John W. Dafoe: The Winnipeg Free Press and Foreign Policy

Peter St. John

Peter St. John (pronounced Sin-jun) taught International Relations at the University of Manitoba for thirty-five years, retiring in 1998. Since his retirement, he has continued to teach, not only at the U of M, but also at the University of Winnipeg, the University of Victoria and St. Andrew's University in Scotland.

     For the past twenty years, he has specialized in Intelligence, Espionage and Terrorism and developed the first course on these subjects in North America. He also taught Middle Eastern Politics and Canadian Foreign Policy.

     In 1996, he won a U of M Outreach award and in 1997 the Stanton Award for Excellence in Teaching.

     He is the author of *Air Piracy, Airport Security and International Terrorism* (1991) and has consulted widely for governments in North America. He also speaks regularly on radio and television, as well as to audiences across Canada and the United States.

     He is married to writer and publisher Barbara Huck and together they have six daughters and two sons, as well as a passel of grandchildren. In 1998, Peter became the Ninth Earl of Orkney

1945–2005

From The Cold War to The New World Order

by Peter St. John

The Post War Years

DURING THE EARLY 1960s, Canadian students studying international relations at the London School of Economics received a break. At the end of one of his lectures, renowned professor Fred S. Northedge announced that students who were interested could attend free lectures at Chatham House, in St. James Square, London. All they had to do was to mention Dr. Northedge's name at the door.

Chatham House had been the home of Prime Minister William Pitt; known as 'Pitt the Younger', he served two terms as Britain's prime minister, from 1783 to 1801 and from 1804 until his death in 1806. Subsequently, this stately mansion became home to the Royal Institute of International Affairs, perhaps the most prestigious organization in the world for the study of international affairs.

As one of Dr. Northedge's students between 1960 and 1964, I attended numerous fascinating talks and lectures there, presented by prime ministers, presidents and other world leaders, including virtually all the newly-elected African heads of state. Among them was President Moise Tshombe of the Congo. In fact, I have a copy of Tshombe's last speech to the institute before he was hijacked and taken to Algiers, where he subsequently died in prison.

There was an interesting rule at Chatham House; members of the audience could use any information gleaned from speakers, as long as that information was not attributed to the speaker. As a result, many speakers felt free to expand on confidential subjects, and communicate ideas to an informed audience, without fear of giving away state secrets.

People from every walk of life and profession belonged to Chatham House over the twentieth century and some of them possessed an extraordinary knowledge and insight. Others made great contributions to British national life. Lord Strang, Nicholas Mansergh and Arnold Toynbee come immediately to mind, also Lionel Curtis, the founder of the famous Round Table Movement.

After World War I, institutes of international affairs grew in both the United States and Canada. Like Britain's Royal Institute, and the U.S. Council on Foreign Relations, the Canadian Institute of International Affairs (CIIA) grew out of the dismay felt by the delegates to the Versailles Peace Conference at the widespread public ignorance of the issues at stake. In her chapter on the origins of the CIIA, Frances Russell has written eloquently on the role of John W. Dafoe in the creation of both the Canadian and Winnipeg branches of the CIIA. Its valuable work of study and education in the field of foreign policy continued through and after World War II and the Cold War period. In 1960, John Wendell Holmes, aged fifty, a retired diplomat and friend and colleague of Lester B. Pearson, took over the helm of the institute as director general. So named because his grandfather hero-worshipped U.S. Supreme Court Justice Oliver Wendell Holmes, John Holmes was an ideal choice to build the Canadian institute. Perhaps he followed Oliver Wendell Holmes' dictum, expressed in *Time* magazine on September 7, 1962, that "Men may come to believe that the ultimate good desired is better reached by free trade in ideas and that truth is the only ground upon which their wishes can be safely carried out."

As president of the CIIA, John Holmes set out "to create an intelligent and informed opinion regarding the international developments that are of vital importance to Canadian welfare." In 1962, after just two-and-a-half years as president, Holmes had attended seven international conferences, visited ten countries and travelled 10,000 miles or 16,000 kilometres in Canada, visiting CIIA branches and lecturing. The organization by then had grown to 2,500 members enrolled in twenty-six branches in every province of Canada save PEI, and also included a branch in New York.

Like other branches, the one in Winnipeg developed study groups (usually numbering ten to fifteen members), received speakers on tour from the national office and conducted its own rigorous pursuit of better understanding international relations and foreign policy. Its members attended the CIIA national conferences, upheld the branch's view at national meetings and above all, travelled all over the world.

It was not by accident that Winnipeg had been called the 'Chicago of the North' at the turn of the twentieth century. The grain trade made the city a hive of international trade activity, producing many knowledgeable businessmen. In addition, the University of Manitoba, later joined by the Universities of Winnipeg and Brandon, attracted both faculty and students deeply interested in international affairs. So, in Winnipeg, 'town and gown' were, on the whole happily intermixed at institute meetings.

John Holmes was nothing if not an evangelist for 'the cause', as he used to call it, and so it was an incredible surprise to me, one day in 1963 as I was teaching in University College London, to receive a letter from him. After introducing himself, he suggested that as a Canadian who had studied in London, I might well be tempted to stay on and teach permanently at "Oxbridge". Instead, he suggested, "Why not consider coming back to Canada, teaching at a Canadian university and especially in the area of Canadian Foreign Policy?" From anyone else it would have been an outrageous invasion of privacy, but from John Holmes it was an idea worth contemplating. He then passed my name on to Professor Richard Hiscocks at the University of Manitoba, and for me, the rest was history. In the fall of 1964, I took up teaching duties at the University of Manitoba.

For anyone interested in joining the RIIA, membership can only be obtained through a unanimous vote of council and I was reluctant to give up such a prestigious membership, for it had taken three years to obtain. But on December 22, 1964, Fred Bancroft, the long time and faithful secretary of the Winnipeg branch wrote in the name of branch chair Alan E. Tarr (son of Edgar Tarr), "We wish to advise that your application of transference of membership to the CIIA, Winnipeg Men's Branch, was approved … on December 18th, 1964."

That year, the Winnipeg institute had a combined membership of 219, with 143 in the men's branch and seventy-six in the women's branch. It was a large and busy organization, and I was to spend the next forty years associated with its membership and meetings.

Frances Russell has painted a brilliant picture of John W. Dafoe and his leadership both in the national office and in the Winnipeg branch's early history. And clearly, it was a healthy and vibrant branch right up to Dafoe's death in 1944. Unfortunately the records between 1945 and 1951 are missing, but it seems evident that the branch was thriving and growing during that period as well. And in 1951, a change occurred that was to enrich the whole Winnipeg learning experience. As Ruth Loutit put it in an interview conducted when she was in her nineties, "We women had had enough and we wanted in." A separate women's branch was created with an executive that included Mrs. W.L. Morton, Mary Dafoe and Marcella Dafoe. Under their leadership, the branch undertook a wide range of activities, including such things as recovering the admittedly shabby furniture at Chatham House! Members of the branch had visited Chatham House in 1952 and, noticing that the chairs and furniture were shoddy and badly in need of a facelift, they initiated a campaign to raise money for recovering the chairs.

This was just the beginning, for almost immediately the women's branch began to plan a joint conference between Winnipeg and the World Affairs Council of Minneapolis. The first conference, on Canadian and U.S. trade barriers (something that still has resonance today) was a resounding success. Alternating between Winnipeg and Minneapolis year by year, the conference became a hugely successful fixture. In 1954, the subject was "Defense and Diplomacy", and in 1955, the "Canadian and U.S. roles in the United Nations". Both groups of women spent the fall and winter months in small study groups, so that by conference time in May, both sides of the border had papers to present on the conference topic.

In 1953, Anne Loutit joined the group. Over the next fifty years, she served as a member and later chair, and assisted by her sister Ruth, helped to revive the combined branch membership in the late 1980s and early 1990s. In fact, Anne Loutit was a member almost to her death at the age of ninety-eight in 2005. By 1954, there were eighty members in the women's branch, and Dorothy Waines, Phyllis Anderson and Dorothy Tarr were also active on the executive.

Like the other branches, Winnipeg helped to fund the national office in Toronto. In 1955, for example, the Winnipeg branch raised $807.06 of which $460 went to the national office, while $337 was retained to run branch activities. A similar ratio persisted for years among most branches. The work of managing the national CIIA was admirably continued in the 1950s by the flexible and thoughtful Edgar MacInnes, a worthy successor to Escott Reid in the 1930s. MacInnes had a combined salary and pension of $12,600 per annum by April 1955, and was ably assisted by Edna Neale, who was then assistant national secretary, later national secretary. She was to be a rock of strength in the CIIA until the late 1980s.

Meanwhile, back in Winnipeg, Mrs. Jewitt was appointed archivist of the women's branch, and a library was started in the University Women's Club at 54 Westgate. This important Winnipeg address was originally the beautiful home of Reverend Charles Gordon — better known by his pen name, Ralph Connor — on the edge of the Assiniboine River near the Misericordia Bridge.

The members must have enjoyed these activies. Indeed, a droll note in the minutes suggests that at least some felt meeting decorum was suffering: "a happy medium between too much entertainment and too much austerity" must be maintained, it reads.

Nevertheless, it's clear that the ladies were allowing no moss to grow. On June 10, 1955, Edgar MacInnes observed that the "Women's Branch is the only one [in Canada] to hold such a joint conference with the U.S." One of the themes was 'get the young people involved' and in 1956 Professors Doug Anglin and Richard Hiscocks were prevailed upon to lead study groups. Not content with educating its own members and the Americans, in 1954–55 the women's branch began a mock UN Assembly for high school students. Better known by its acronym, MUNA, this organization continued through most of the rest of the century.

In January 1957, the women's branch planned an international conference on "Diplomacy and Foreign Policy" without the help of the national office. The keynote speaker, Mike Pearson, soon to be prime minister, was slated to speak at the Playhouse Theatre. And reflecting how busy the future Nobel Laureate might be, the minutes record that "if Mr Pearson is unable to come due to pressure of world events, the text of his speech will be read to the audience by a local person."

Throughout the balance of the decade, the conferences were both well attended and varied in their focus. The 1958 conference drew more than 100 people and a year later Justice Samuel Freedman spoke on Israel, while noted historian W.L. (Bill) Morton chaired the event in 1960. At all these events, the formal presentations were followed by 'hash sessions', freewheeling discussions in which the members from Minneapolis — "our Southern friends" as they were called in the minutes — were robust participants. And it's clear that visits between the two cities went both ways. In 1960 a member of the Winnipeg executive stated that if the conference with Minneapolis was held on a certain date in May that she would "regretfully have to tender her resignation since it clashed with the opera in Minneapolis."

In 1960, Florence Jones, Dorothy Tarr, Robena Whiteside, Mrs F.S. Manor and Ruth McClintock and Kirk Wright appear as active members in the executive minutes and in February, Professor Fred Soward, well known as a dean of Canadian foreign policy, spoke to the branch.

The following January, John Holmes paid his first visit to the joint executives at 54 Westgate and Anne Loutit became chair of the women's institute in the same year. That fall, the branch held a conference on 'The Communist World'. Thoughtful as ever, the women's executive presented corsages to their members embarking on long or significant journeys.

Muriel Smith joined the executive in the spring of 1961 and remained active into the twenty-first century. In an interview in March 2005, Smith, who subsequently pursued a distinguished career in politics and become the first female deputy premier in Canada, commented on the Minneapolis-Winnipeg conferences. She recalled how striking it was that the Americans were much less willing to speak out because of McCarthyism, while the Canadians were quite freewheeling and critical. One can just imagine the impact on the Winnipeg community that this group of highly articulate women must have had.

The women's branch at the time had ninety-two members, which may have been its zenith; in the decades to come, women would begin to move into the work force in numbers previously unseen during peace time. Juggling jobs, children and life at home, they found the time needed to participate in study groups was greatly reduced.

Records are not available for the men's branch of the institute between 1945 and 1960. Perhaps they are languishing in someone's basement; maybe they are lost forever. That we have any record at all is due to the orderly collection of minutes and excellent bookkeeping on the part of Dave and Roquelle Ross. The latter was a member of the women's group and the former looked after the minutes for the men's branch for many years as secretary, following in the footsteps of another model of efficiency, Fred Bancroft. Always present, always pleasant, highly informed, the Rosses demonstrated how international affairs could become a consuming passion. As a result, their orderly habits now inform our understanding of the period. The pinnacle of the men's branch membership appears to have been reached in 1960–61 when there were 171 members. Across Canada, the total CIIA membership was 2,439. Allan Tarr was chair of Winnipeg's men's group in the early 1960s, clearly having walked in the footsteps of his father, Edgar Tarr. A pleasant man, and well informed, he ran the branch efficiently, with Fred Bancroft as faithful secretary for many years. Despite their best efforts, the membership of the men's branch began a slow but steady decline in the 1960s.

In 1962–63 the men's branch had slipped to 145 members; two years later there were 121, and by 1967–68 just 103. Despite the downward trend, the 1960s was, in retrospect, notable for the sheer distinction of the membership. In 1963, for example, Christopher Dafoe, grandson of John W. Dafoe, joined. Representing the academics were Murray S. Donnelly, John W. Dafoe's biographer; Cornelius J. Jaenen, who was later to cut a swath at Université d'Ottawa; Bill Morton, the distinguished Canadian historian; Hugh L.

Saunderson and Doug Chevrier, respectively president and registrar of the University of Manitoba, along with Dean of Arts Bill Waines and Dean of Agriculture J. Clay Gilson. Others, from government, included Deputy Minister Stuart J. Anderson, Saul Cherniack, later a minister in the first Manitoba NDP government and Stanley Knowles, long time MP and legendary figure in the NDP nationally. Sidney Spivak, leader of the Manitoba Conservatives and later senator, and Senator T.A. Crerar were also members, as was Gordon MacDonell, president of the UN Association.

Representing the legal profession were Justice Samuel Freedman, later Chief Justice of Manitoba; Walter C. Newman, QC, founder of the well known law firm; Justice C. Rhodes Smith; G.P.R. Tallin, QC, later Chief Justice; Alan Sweatman of Thompson Dorfman Sweatman; B.B. Dubienski, QC, and Judge W.J. Lindal. From the business community were Sol Kanee; E.B. and Gordon P. Osler; Wilf Queen-Hughes of *The Winnipeg Tribune*; Richard S. Malone, publisher of the *Winnipeg Free Press* and Fred S. Manor of the paper's editorial board, and Charles and Guy Croft. Finally, there was a sprinkling of well known doctors such as Dr. P.H.T. Thorlakson, founder of the Winnipeg Clinic; Dr. Jim Nixon-Briggs, pediatrician; Dr. Louis Cherniak, father of Saul; Dr. Charles Hollenberg; Dr. Alan A. Klass; Dr. B.H. Lyons; and Dr. Arthur Majury. In short, the membership list might have been an honour roll of distinguished Winnipeggers and the elevated level of discussion made CIIA meetings exciting experiences.

Arriving in Winnipeg in the fall of 1964, I was immediately impressed with the institute, for most meetings drew more than 100 members. After dinner, chairs would be pushed back and the speaker given up to an hour to make his case. There then followed critical questioning, sometimes quite competitive, always stimulating, which could also last up to an hour. Finally, the speaker would be thanked and taken for a well-earned drink or back to his hotel, usually the venerable Fort Garry.

Despite these scintillating sessions, the declining membership was a matter of continuing concern to the branch. In retrospect, I believe the reasons for the decline were demographic and structural and had much to do with the emergence of television. Nevertheless, there were new young members including, in 1964, Professor Lloyd Axworthy, who would one day be Canada's foreign minister; Harry Walsh, the famous criminal lawyer; Harry Mardon, city editor of *The Winnipeg Tribune*, and Brigadier J.E.C. Pangman. Meetings were held at the Chamber of Commerce building that year and included several brilliant and timely performances. Professor Bill Morton spoke on: 'Is Canada one Nation or two', while Professor Laurier

Lapierre gave an address on 'French Canada looks at the World'. French Ambassador Jean Ethier-Blais spoke so well on 'France and Gaullism' (remember this was prior to 1967 and President de Gaulle's famous "Vive le Québec Libre"), that the secretary was prompted to send a note to the National Office describing it as "an exceptionally good meeting". It was high praise indeed from Fred Bancroft.

The following year, 1965, was a bumper year in terms of speakers. In January, Sir John Slessor, Marshall of the Royal Air Force, spoke on 'The Atlantic Community and the Problem of Nuclear Control', and in the same month Ernesto F. Betancourt, an army officer who had broken with Fidel Castro, spoke on 'New Developments in the Cuban Problem'. In May, Escott Reid (who, as the previous chapter outlines, had been the first executive director of the CIIA) spoke on 'The World Bank in Operation'. Other speakers included Israeli Ambassador Gershon Asher and French Ambassador François Leduc. The latter spoke on 'French Foreign Policy', but only on condition of strict confidentiality. A telegram to the branch stated that "M. Leduc is prepared to be quite frank, but the rules of the Institute must be strictly observed in every respect." The meeting was packed.

In the summer of 1965, the CIIA National Office held its third Annual Banff Conference on International Development on the subject of 'Canada's Role as a Middle Power'. King Gordon, Ralph Connor's son, convened the conference and hundreds of CIIA members, including many from Winnipeg, converged on Banff. It was a spectacular success, with intense discussion and argument about the continuing use of "middlepowermanship" as Canada's foreign policy. Prime Minister Lester B. Pearson graced the conference with his presence and a speech, but not until after his car was delayed by prostrate Vietnam demonstrators — including King Gordon's daughter — who were lying on the road.

Over the three days of the conference, informal groupings of distinguished Canadians could be seen dotted about the Banff Conference Centre. At one point, I found myself in a small group with the prime minister and John Holmes, who were reminiscing about the Suez Crisis, which had resulted in Pearson's Nobel Prize; John Holmes had been his vital contact person in Ottawa. They laughed and joked about something that for me was already the stuff of legend. But there was confrontation, too. A movement from the floor challenged Canada's middle power role, and especially the brand of Quiet Diplomacy practiced by former Canadian Ambassador to the U.S. Arnold Heeney. The forces of revolution were led by Lloyd Axworthy; when he and I appeared on CBC television criticizing the middle power role, we were dismissed as "those youth in sweaters". Though a series of resolutions challenging Canada's middle power role were passed in the conference plenary session, the book that emerged the following year, *Canada's Role as a Middle Power*, bore no reference to the conference's self-criticism movement. Nevertheless, the exercise illustrated brilliantly the stimulating nature of CIIA activities in the mid-1960s as the Vietnam War gathered steam.

In August 1965, the executive set about some serious attempts at revitalizing the branch; Cornelius Jaenen and I were approached to chair a committee to build up the membership. Earlier, at the Banff Conference, I had spent an afternoon and demolished several beers with the feisty *Winnipeg Tribune* journalist who chaired the Winnipeg branch, Wilf Queen-Hughes. Wilf was a good natured, combative and articulate student of international affairs. He had been in the hopeless siege of Hong Kong, and a prisoner of war for several years there. Suddenly, in the warm Banff air, he had an attack of malaria. Pouring perspiration for half an hour, he talked at length about Hong Kong. I was quite unused to such symptoms, but he assured me the spell would pass, and it did. However, I never forgot his description of being a Japanese prisoner of war.

Wilf Queen-Hughes and I became firm friends and it was undoubtedly because of that meeting that I, "a young man with a refreshingly enthusiastic approach to life," as I was once described in a notice that went out to members, was asked to address the question of membership at the national CIIA meeting in Vancouver in the fall of 1965.

That same fall, Director General John Holmes paid a week-long visit to the University of Manitoba. He had been invited by Professor Bill Morton, who was Provost of University College, to spend a week in residence as the college's first Visitor in Residence. Among many other commitments that week, John Holmes spoke to my fledgling Canadian Foreign Policy class. For me and my students, it was a memorable experience, for Holmes was a great internationalist and he just happened at the time to be writing the last words of his soon to be published book, *The Better Part of Valour*. One of the students in that Canadian Foreign Policy class was Stan Carlson, who went into External Affairs after university and later married Margaret Catley. They were the first External Affairs officers ever to marry and, posted in Ottawa and New York respectively, met on the Canadian-American border on weekends while conducting their courtship. (Later, in the 1990s, Stan was in charge of the Peacekeeping Crisis Centre at the UN, while Margaret Catley-Carlson, then president of the World Population Council, gave the keynote address at the 1999 Pan Am Games International

Women's Conference; that address is reproduced in this book.) In addition to speaking engagements at the university, John Holmes met to discuss the future of the CIIA with the executives of the local men's and women's branches.

Between 1965 and 1967 much heated discussion took place over the U.S. role in Vietnam and what Canada's role should be. This led John Holmes to write a penetrating account about how the Americans got into Vietnam. The article, in the CIIA's *International Journal*, illustrated the CIIA's teaching role in international affairs.

There were always tensions between the national office and the local branches, particularly in Western Canada. Inevitably, as with London's Chatham House, the national office became the focus of the institute's activities while the branches, though fed regular speakers, were gradually left to develop their own programs. As a result, success depended largely on local leadership. Wilf Queen-Hughes was such a leader. Originally named Hughes, he added the prefix to his surname when he married Gloria Queen, the daughter of a former mayor of Winnipeg. Gloria and Wilf Queen-Hughes lived in a large, rambling white house at 697 Wellington Crescent and frequently held institute or executive meetings there. Wilf would often invite speakers and members back to his home for a drink after downtown branch meetings. He remained chair until 1966 and when he died several years later, he left an interesting bequest in his will. Administered by the Winnipeg Foundation, the bequest left an annual sum of money to invite a distinguished guest to be flown in to speak to the branch. Though the non-attribution rule continued to prevail at Queen-Hughes Lectures, over the past decade or so, a number of Queen-Hughes lecturers proved willing to allow their presentations to be published. The result can be seen in this book and is perhaps a fitting tribute to Wilf Queen-Hughes' vision and generosity, not to mention his commitment to international education.

As a result of John Holmes' visit in 1965, I was put in touch with the External Affairs Visiting Diplomat Speakers Program. For the rest of the century, a stream of diplomats came at External Affairs' (later Foreign Affairs') expense to speak to generations of students at the University of Manitoba. More often than not, these speakers would be shared with the University of Winnipeg and frequently they would then address the local branch of the CIIA. It was a wonderful education system that produced a knowledgeable and interested body of foreign affairs devotees in Winnipeg. And, on a more personal note, it contributed to the fact that over the years at least thirty of my students went into External Affairs to become diplomats, adding prestige to the both the city and the university.

In 1966, Professor Reuben Bellan became chair of the Winnipeg branch and an excerpt from his letter to the executive committee went as follows:

> I have been greatly honoured in being asked to assume the chairmanship of the Winnipeg Branch of the Canadian Institute of International Affairs; the Branch has a deeply respected tradition and its chairmen have been distinguished members of the Winnipeg community. I hope that the confidence shown in me will not prove misplaced and that I will adequately fulfil the responsibilities of the office.
>
> Foremost among these I consider to be the obligation to ensure that the Institute enrols all those men who would be desirable members and that its meetings are stimulating, informative and well-attended. All chairmen of course have felt this obligation; the different times and circumstances in which they held office required differing approaches and procedures which had to be worked out afresh in each case.
>
> I have called a meeting of the Executive at which we can consider together what policies and measures would be currently most appropriate and would enable us to achieve our goals in amplest measure. Please come to contribute to the discussion.

Among the first speakers under Bellan's watch were William Barton, later Canadian Ambassador to the United Nations, and the great British traveller, author and guru to Prince Charles, Laurens Van der Post, who spoke on 'The Current African Situation'. Among those in the audience for Van der Post's lecture was a young Ugandan student named Dent Ocaya-Lackidi, who won the Faculty of Arts gold medal at the University of Manitoba, before returning to Uganda to teach at Makerere College, later University, and to write for the paper in Kampala. Because his newspaper pieces were often critical of Idi Amin, he was hunted down and driven out of Uganda, barely escaping with his life.

Another student member in 1966 was Colin Robertson, who went on to a distinguished career in Foreign Affairs, serving in New York, Hong Kong and Los Angeles as Canadian Consul, before becoming Canada's

Minister (Advocacy) to the U.S. Congress in Washington. He was among those who agreed to allow his Queen-Hughes lecture to be published; it can be found on page 72.

In 1967, Canada's centennial year, Lloyd Axworthy resigned from the local branch to embark on a career in politics that would include a number of years as Canada's minister of Foreign Affairs. His commitment to the CIIA continues, however, and one of his recent lectures, given as president of the University of Winnipeg, is included in this book, on page 180.

Despite the efforts of the various executive members, the excellence of the speakers and the immediacy of many of their topics, membership continued its slow slide. In 1968, the national office observed cryptically that thirteen branches across the country had less than sixty-five members on their rolls.

Following two years of study in England, I became branch chair in 1971, but perhaps more importantly for this publication, David Ross had become secretary; he was to continue the fine tradition established for so many years by Fred Bancroft. In a long memo announcing a December 6, 1972 executive meeting to discuss the future of the branch, Ross wrote a prescient paragraph which, in retrospect, explained the problem of declining membership.

> It should be noted that there is an undercurrent of opinion to the effect that travel opportunity available to large sections of people, the proliferation of speaker's programmes on university campuses, [and] the frequent appearances on television of persons prominent in international affairs all contribute to redundancy of the traditional CIIA programme. Moreover, past and present members with special expertise in this discipline no longer find stimulation in the level of insights available through participation in branch activity. The net result is a downward spiral of satisfaction. It is generally felt therefore: if it has outlived its usefulness, it should be allowed a dignified exit. A silent majority in this situation signalizes concurrence in this gloomy prospect. The next few months should be conclusive.

In spite of such doom and gloom, the branch was to last another thirty years.

In April 1973, a memo circulated to executive members mentioned several interesting developments. First, the total membership of ninety-two (fifty-three men and thirty-nine women) was better than that of many branches across the country. Second, Secretary Ross reported the establishment of the Wilf Queen-Hughes Memorial Fund. And finally, the memo announced the women's joint conference with the Twin Cities (Minneapolis-St. Paul) World Affairs Council, which was scheduled for the University Women's Club, with a reception at Government House by the lieutenant governor. Twenty years after its inception, the women were still celebrating their foreign policy relationship with Minneapolis.

In 1974, under the new chair, Dr. Bernard Hoffman, the impressive program of speakers included U.S. Ambassador William J. Porter; British High Commissioner Sir John Johnston; the former president of the Canadian Labour Congress Donald MacDonald, and Canada's Secretary of State for External Affairs Allan McEachen. Colin Robertson, who was working at the time as McEachen's personal assistant, told us that it was his first foreign policy speech after assuming the post.

In 1976, a University of Manitoba history professor, Lovell Clark, became chair, and his tenure began with a November lecture so brilliant that I can still recall its impact nearly thirty years later. Dr. John Greer Nicholson spoke on 'A Russian Looks at the Outside World'. A fluent speaker of Russian, Nicholson was chair of the Department of Slavic Studies at McGill University, had served with the British Intelligence Corps and had made numerous visits to Russia. His view of the Russian character was so fascinating that none of us ever thought the same way again about the U.S.S.R. In the space of an hour or two, he had forever changed our stereotypical perceptions.

Just a couple of weeks later, Jack W. Pickersgill, former private secretary to Mackenzie King, spoke on 'Prime Minister St. Laurent and the Cold War'. It was like stepping back into Canadian history and reliving the most intense years of the Cold War.

In 1978, my own life changed substantially, largely because of an invitation from the national branch of the CIIA to lecture across Canada on a subject that I had begun to teach at the University of Manitoba — 'Intelligence, Espionage and Terrorism', popularly known as 'Spies and Lies'.

The tour gave me a window on many CIIA branches across the nation, including Saint John, Fredericton, Montréal, Sherbrooke, Lennoxville, Ottawa, Hamilton, St. Catherine's, Windsor, London, Thunder Bay, Regina, Saskatoon, Calgary, Edmonton, Vancouver and Victoria. Thereafter I spoke regularly to many of the branches, some of them several times, which gave quite an interesting picture of the CIIA stretching across northern North

America. Some branches seemed to have a somewhat tenuous existence, while others like Ottawa, Toronto, Montreal and Victoria had particularly large memberships. Total CIIA membership was 3,194 in 1981-82, but had declined by 1986-87 to 2,743, at which time overall membership numbers ceased to be published in the CIIA annual report.

One gained a sense of how a branch was doing within minutes of landing in a community, because members almost invariably began discussing local problems. Nevertheless, even smaller branches often had lively meetings and many branches interacted with others nearby. There was quite a lot of traffic between Winnipeg, Regina and Saskatoon, and Winnipeg and Thunder Bay. Occasionally this led to member exchanges or a joint conference, and it certainly created a connection between executives.

These CIIA tours led to hundreds of interviews on radio and television, beginning about 1980. But in view of the non-partisan approach of the institute and since I was frequently critical of government, it seemed better to identify with the University of Manitoba than with the CIIA. Professor Rhais Khan, who was chair of the Winnipeg branch several times, often spoke on the Middle East to the media and was always identified with the University of Winnipeg, rather than the CIIA. Lloyd Axworthy was also interviewed hundreds of times, particularly after he became Foreign Minister in the 1990s and worked on both the Landmines Treaty and an agenda of Human Security. Lloyd always spoke as a university faculty member, a member of parliament or as a minister of the Crown. Colin Robertson was another frequent speaker to CIIA branches, and as he became more senior, his messages became more weighty. However, Colin never spoke as a member of the CIIA. Nor did Nelson Wiseman, professor of political science professor at the University of Toronto and a gifted commentator on Canadian politics. A product of the University of Manitoba, who had his thesis supervised by John Holmes himself, Wiseman was always associated with the U of T. Perhaps Ruth Loutit was the one member of the Winnipeg branch who wore the label of the institute most persistently. For nearly thirty years she spoke on the United Nations and related themes weekly on her program on Public Cable Television on Winnipeg's Channel 13. Had others been more regularly identified with the CIIA, the institute itself might have benefitted. The point, however, was that institute members used their knowledge for public education.

Every branch across the country had members who could have spoken articulately about international issues on radio or television, just as members did during the 1930s. The CBC or other stations could have balanced their journalistic coverage, particularly on radio, with an informed and informative series that might have shed light on complex or incendiary subjects such as the violence in the Middle East or, later, 9/11. Members of the media tend to dwell on tragedies and disasters without attempting to explain why these things happen. CIIA membership gives people the background knowledge that the media can not, or does not, give the public.

When Jacques Rastoul became national director of the CIIA in 1979, there was a real possibility of creating public education on the Middle East, for Rastoul was a personable, knowledgeable and outgoing scholar of the region. In February 1979, he toured Western Canada, speaking to all the branches on 'Towards a Palestinian-Israeli Settlement'. The level of discussion in CIIA meetings on this topic showed that the attentive opinion in Canada was streets ahead of the superficial media coverage. After a four-month, ten-country research trip around ten Middle Eastern countries in 1982, I too was convinced that peace was possible and a talk given in October 1982 in Winnipeg called 'Muddle, Mystique and Mephistophiles in the Middle East' was taken right across Canada. In Winnipeg, a popular and constructive CBC phone-in program called Questionnaire frequently addressed the Middle Eastern problem in an intelligent and educative manner, but these themes came and went at the whim of individual producers. One wonders if CBC personnel might not themselves benefit from some immersion in CIIA-type education in order to gain a balance on the more intractable problems in international affairs.

Between 1979 and 1981 the Middle East and terrorism were well addressed at CIIA meetings under the chairmanship of Rhais Khan. Also during his tenure, the women's group merged with the men's group under the leadership of Anne M. Loutit, one of the earliest members of the institute.

In the early 1980s, David McDonald, an editorial writer with the *Winnipeg Free Press*, chaired the Winnipeg branch but left no records or minutes when he left the city. Meetings of a high quality continued, though with reduced membership, and two of these were typically effective. In May 1983, Egyptian Ambassador Tahseen Basheer spoke on the 'Challenge of Peace in the Middle East'. It was a masterful speech by an Arab Harvard graduate who had served as official Egyptian spokesman under both Nasser and Sadat. Of Alexandrine origin, he spoke brilliantly and informatively, making such a compelling mark that one can remember the speech twenty years later.

In the latter part of the decade, Reuben Bellan again chaired the branch, before the group gradually faded into history as the century turned.

Chairs Mark Kubanek (1991), Ken Emmond (1992), Vince de Rose (1993), Kathleen Burke (1994–95), myself (1996–98), and Rhais Khan steered a branch of dwindling members into the twenty-first century. Some of the more memorable addresses were in April 1991, by Canada's extremely articulate ambassador to the U.S.S.R., Vern Turner, on 'Prospects for the Soviet Union'. In November 1993, Kim Nossal, a McMaster University professor and former student of John Holmes, spoke to the branch on 'Accidental Statesman'. In May 1993, a Queen-Hughes lecture was given by Pearson biographer John English on 'The Legacy of Pearsonian Internationalism'. A year later, U of T Professor Jack Granatstein spoke to the branch on 'Canadian Generals in Canadian Foreign Policy'. In June 1994, Canada's former ambassador to Japan and NATO, John Halstead, gave the Queen-Hughes lecture on 'The Foreign and Defence Policy Reviews' and in September, former CBC broadcaster and author Knowlton Nash spoke on 'A Look Back at Canada–U.S. Relations'. A number of the speakers who addressed the branch in its last decade have allowed their presentations to be reproduced in this book.

However, by the turn of the twenty-first century five members of the branch were in their nineties, and though an aggressive pursuit of student members continued, many student members left the city and the branch in pursuit of graduate studies elsewhere. One can only hope that our loss was another branch's gain.

The pressure of life for young families in the 1990s tended to militate against young professionals coming for a supper meeting at 6 p.m. after a long day at work. Lunch-hour meetings, often at the Manitoba Legislature did not fare any better. And as mentioned earlier, the combined educative power of both television and the internet tended to keep people in their homes, especially during a harsh Winnipeg winter. However, this story would be incomplete without mentioning two last institute attempts at public education.

On December 13, 1996, a Foreign Policy Consultation took place in Winnipeg under the guidance of Foreign Minister Lloyd Axworthy. The paper on which this 'Citizen's Forum' was based, aiming to come up with new thinking on foreign policy, was written by former Undersecretary of State J.W. (Si) Taylor. Taylor himself was from Winnipeg originally and his paper is reproduced in this book. Breaking into separate groups, debating new directions in foreign policy and then coming back into plenary session was a creative attempt by the foreign minister to produce in a city the old German practice of *landsgemeinde*, or 'village pump democracy'. This kind of consultation was to give a grass roots thrust to Lloyd Axworthy's Human

Security agenda. The meetings in several cities across Canada were sponsored by the CIIA.

In the following fall of 1997, a large CIIA conference on Canada and Asia took place in Regina with several hundred people present. The Honourable Joe Clark and the Honourable Lloyd Axworthy spoke at the conference as did Saskatchewan Premier Roy Romanow. The national office sent a busload of students west from Toronto and in Winnipeg twenty-one additional students climbed onto the bus accompanied by Ruth Loutit, who was well into her eighties, but whose interest in international affairs gave no sign of flagging. They were all a great presence at the conference, which turned out to be hugely educative on Canadian-Asian relations.

During the final years of the Winnipeg branch, membership gradually dwindled from the forties in the 1990s to about fifteen or twenty at the turn of the century. In such circumstances it was difficult to get a quorum for meetings and so at last the Winnipeg branch of the CIIA passed into history. For almost seventy years the Winnipeg branch of the CIIA taught, cajoled, discussed, occasionally argued and always evaluated the critical moments in Canadian foreign policy and world events — what finer tradition to bequeath to the cause of national and international education.

JOHN WENDELL HOLMES

John Holmes was a diplomat, teacher, public educator and author who worked with the Department of External Affairs from 1943 to 1960. He served in New York, London and Moscow, before retiring as assistant undersecretary of state for External Affairs.

Between 1960 and 1977, he directed the Canadian Institute of International Affairs, and concurrently taught Canadian Foreign Policy, first at York University and later at the University of Toronto, where he was appointed professor of International Relations. He authored numerous books, including T*he Better Part of Valour; Canada: A Middle-Aged Power; The Shaping of Peace* (two volumes) and *Life With Uncle*.

John Holmes was largely responsible for both designing and later explaining Canada's role as peacekeeper and middle power. He died in August 1988 at the age of seventy-eight. The John Holmes Library at the CIIA's national office in Toronto is named for him.

This chapter was originally part of a foreign policy text, *Mackenzie King to Philosopher King*, edited by Peter St. John, which was published in 1986.

1986

The World According to Ottawa

by John W. Holmes

To BEGIN WITH it is well to bear in mind that the foreign policy, and more particularly the diplomacy, of a middle power is generically different from that of a great power, let alone a superpower. Canada can have by its own choice policies with basic aims similar to those of the United States or Britain or Germany and parallel or coincidental with them, and it largely has. Its methods of pursuing those aims, however, its way of gaining its ends and using its influence, must be quite different. As most of the arguments among allies are about ways and means, this differentiation is important. The much greater dependence of the weaker power on international institutions, for example, leads to differing priorities, as on the Law of the Sea. Furthermore, the lesser power's policies must be more reactive, more easily adaptable. It must live with situations that are rarely of its making. Whatever Canadians may have thought of U.S. policy in Vietnam, for example, their calculations as to what they should do had to be based on American policy as it was, not as they would have preferred it to be. Accepting perforce is not the same as agreeing. United States policy towards the People's Republic of China shaped the issue for the world at large, including Canada. Canada, with other like-minded countries and in the U.N., tried with varying degrees of success to help avert an American-Chinese confrontation. In the end, Canada had not so much a decisive as a catalytic effect on the question, for it recognized the People's Republic at a moment when many other countries were ready to move.

Canada does not get far with simple denunciation as a tactic and is inclined, therefore, to keep relatively quiet and see what can be made of a situation, however lamentable. To do anything at all, it must have allies or associates, unless, as is sometimes the case, it has a natural role as intermediary because it has no direct interest. As its powers of persuasion are in most cases limited, it must carefully calculate what kind of leverage it could exert in each case and which kind of diplomacy is likely to be effective. It is not true that Canadian diplomacy is always quiet. The trouble is that when it is loud, only Canadians seem to be listening. Perhaps it is intended to calm them.

Canada's foreign policy is a product of its own geography and its own history. This is more a matter of instinct than conscious calculation. Internal critics argue sometimes for a drastic alteration of Canada's position in the world. It is an argument that might make sense for a country in outer space, but is instinctively rejected by those in charge, who know — or just feel — that it would not work. By situation and upbringing, Canadians are members of the Western community and tend, perhaps regrettably, to see the world in roughly the same way as Dutchmen or Ohioans. If they agree with their allies on basics, it is not under constraint. Nevertheless, Canadian geography and Canadian history, and consequently Canadian foreign policy, vary in notable ways from those of other North American and North Atlantic countries.

The Ambiguities of Geography

There is the elemental fact that Canada is the second-largest country in the world. A small and scattered population trying to control a gigantic mass of land and water is bound to a perpetual state of insecurity. Hence the habitual cautiousness of Canadian foreign policy, as distinct from Canadian diplomacy, which has at times been boldly imaginative. The irony is that Canada is itself the product of grandiose fantasy. How did we get the reputation for canniness? The extension of sovereignty from sea to sea a century ago, in defiance of a great power, with no internal means of communication between far-flung pockets of settlement, may have been the rashest act of nation-building in history. It makes the celebrated union of thirteen colonies look pretty tame. Whether or not that act was justified may well be questioned by other countries, who could see it as an act either of usurpation or sheer irresponsibility. That old sourpuss, Goldwin Smith, thought it was — and he was probably right. One might say that Canada exhausted itself in one mad act of creation and its foreign (as well as its domestic) policy is a matter of coping with the consequences ever since. So much for our regarding ourselves as victims of the great powers.

The Canadian predicament is perhaps best illustrated in the dilemma of a defence policy. The defence of Canada is mind-boggling, and Canadians are still boggled by it. And rightly so. Some form of collective defence has always been the inescapable answer. To defend the new dominion 100 years ago Canada had to call on the reluctant British. To defend itself now it must rely on collective defence with its NATO allies, and in particular, of course, the United States. Having grown up reasonably secure in a triangle, balancing greater powers against each other, Canadians have a historic instinct for principles of deterrence and counterweight. Those who were planning Canada's postwar strategies talked about its 'alliance potential'. It is not that Canadians simplistically expect others to defend them, although they certainly like to keep their contribution at the least expensive level. To say that the United States is expected to defend Canada is not quite right. Canadians see it as defence by an alliance into which each country contributes according to its means. The theory can be maintained even though there is legitimate argument as to whether a member is paying its fair share.

From a Canadian perspective, it was Canadians who realized sooner than Americans that they had to play their part in an Atlantic security system. That is why they went to war voluntarily in 1914 and 1939 and subsequently took a lead in promoting a North Atlantic alliance. Pearl Harbour did not happen to Canada. The very different ways in which Canada and the United States entered the two world wars have left different instinctive attitudes toward the way in which wars start and the extent to which joining up is a matter of choice. There is the persistent assumption that the Canadian contribution is supplementary rather than initial or decisive. It is at least a century since Canada has itself been a *casus belli* — or almost.

The maintenance of sovereignty over the vast northern regions must be constantly demonstrated and it is an enormous area to patrol, let alone populate. When the United States itself has reservations about Canada's claims to sovereignty in the Arctic regions, there is an additional reason for Canada to carry its own end of the responsibility for continental defence. The new economic zones must be policed by Canadians, although reciprocal agreements with fishing states (except the United States) have made this less arduous than expected. The cost of fool-proof defence is staggering and the smaller country is less able to risk extravagant miscalculation — as on the Arrow aircraft in the 1950s, for example. There is a constant temptation to say that as the country cannot be defended there is no point wasting money in trying. The only practical alternative for defence has seemed to be the alliance policy of deterrence. Though some articulate Canadian nationalists hanker after an independent neutralism, it is a nationalistic instinct of another kind to avert the necessity of excessive American participation in the defence of northern North America by keeping Canadian defences above a certain minimum. This is the kind of required double vision that has been labelled 'defence against help'.

The failure of Canadians to define a satisfactory strategic policy or to produce a native school of strategic thinking may to some extent be attributed to the difficulty of producing a rational strategy for an irrationally conceived country. The Canadian tendency since the Second World War to take a comparatively less dramatic view of Soviet intentions is largely attributable to the variant approaches of the Ottawa bureaucrats to the Cold War, but one suspects it has been accepted willingly by politicians who are tempted to take a chance rather than face the impossible questions. The ultimate decision about war is not theirs. The rationality of collective defence through NATO to keep aggressors away is accepted, but the public finds the reasoning elusive. It is not easy to grasp and hold the reason for keeping a token but cost-efficient force in the Rhineland rather than doing something more to cope with the enormous Canadian frontier.

Canada has always insisted that NATO comprises two continents and is not a North American aid to Europe scheme, that withdrawing troops from Europe to Canada would not be withdrawing them from the common defence. The Arctic is a vital part of the grand allied strategy. Canada is twice the size of NATO Europe and the U.S.S.R. is 'up here' not 'over there'. The maintenance of communications and an infrastructure in the North, whether military or civilian, does in some Canadian eyes form a contribution that compensates — to some extent at least — for their relatively poor performance in the provision of conventional NATO forces.

Another reason for worry about sheer size is that Canada owns so much real estate when the pressure of population on resources in the world at large is the major threat to the kind of world order Canada very much needs. For Canada, more so than for most lesser powers, security threats are perceived not in the aggressive postures of neighbours but in the disruption of the international equilibrium that is so important to a land unusually dependent upon commerce and usurping a lot of space. This instinctive concern for a favourable balance of power accounts, to some extent, for Canada's going to war in 1914 and 1939. The sense of insecurity is aggravated by a guilty awareness of the inequality Canadians enjoy and the vague menace of adjustment. Canadians sometimes suggest that they play a more useful and appropriate part in aid and development than in military defence and that that is their best form of contribution to peace and stability. That might make sense in a sensible world.

Anxiety about population has always been central in Canadian foreign policy, although it is not a subject usually included elsewhere in the classic themes of foreign policy. The first Canadian official representative abroad was an immigration agent, and there were immigration, as well as trade, representatives around the world years before Canada got round to establishing its own diplomatic service. Immigration represents a paradox. The country has always felt the need of a larger internal market and of sufficient population to satisfy the requirements of a vast land. On the other hand reserving the historic ethnic balance and traditional cultural values, not to mention concerns about employment, provoke a constant anxiety to control the flow. As a good UN and Commonwealth member, the government has eliminated racial distinctions for immigrants, but has not, needless to say, pressed the People's Republic of China to allow unrestricted emigration. Although Canadians are somewhat guiltily conscious of owning so much land, they believe that the arable land is now being exploited and that the perception of Canada on a map as limitless acreage is misleading. As the problems of urban areas grow and the environmentalists hold sway, the enthusiasm for a vaster population has diminished. Nevertheless, contemplation of the population statistics for Asia or Latin America are unnerving.

The possession of natural resources does give Canadians a certain self-confidence. The need to sell resources to counterbalance the import of manufactures from other countries is recognized, but there is a persistent fear that the resources are expendable. A feeling that the United States has forged ahead on its own resources in the past century and exhausted them has induced in Canada an anxiety to hang on to its own non-renewable resources for a greater industrial future. Hence the suspicion of proposals for North American accords or continental resource plans.

Canada, unlike even the largest powers, has a three ocean frontier as well as an enormous land and water boundary, and is required, therefore, to have an awareness *à tous azimuts*. Suffice it to note here the increasing pressures of geographical exposure, especially on a country that grew up in relative security behind the shelter of the Anglo-American entente and an impenetrable ice cap. A persistent Canadian dilemma is that there really ought to be a great power in its strategic situation. The enormity of the land and the fragility of the infrastructure account for the perpetual nervousness of Canadian foreign policy and also for what must seem to outsiders curious gyrations of public opinion from a modesty that is positively irresponsible to expectations of influence beyond that of either superpower. It is and it isn't the world's second largest power.

The term middle power, which Canadian policy makers and policy describers began to use in the postwar period, was primarily intended to define the right of lesser powers on functional grounds to play major or minor roles depending on their specific capacity in the particular subject matter. It was intended also as a discipline for a people who tended to measure themselves alongside the two great powers between which they had existed and were inclined either to see themselves as helpless or to overestimate the scope for their diplomacy. The term at first had to do with size and capacity, but as intermediary states were required for peacekeeping and arbitrating by the UN, and the middling countries filled the bill, the term developed an ambiguity. Whereas the possession of great military or economic power can perversely be an advantage in some kinds of diplomacy, the lesser power can be trusted because it has no direct involvement, and because it is less intimidating and seems therefore less of a threat. In the provision of aid and development, its motives are less suspect (though by no means entirely so) because what is offered is rarely of sufficient consequence to influence the internal politics of the recipient. It often is more beloved (or less disliked) not for superior virtue or unselfishness but because it hasn't the capacity for malevolence. Neither has it, of course, the same capability of protecting, aiding and abetting.

The neat concept of middlepowermanship helped Canadians through the transition from a passive to an active role in world affairs, but a reaction set in at home in the Sixties. Abroad, Young Lochinvar was acquiring resentments and wider competition in the mediatory game. There has, mercifully, been less chatter in recent years about role-playing, but Canadian diplomacy, nevertheless, has retained a natural bent for "helpful fixing" and a consequent instinct to stand off a little from issues in order to fix and help if required. Peacekeeping, which was the most dramatic expression of middlepowermanship, did satisfy a certain Canadian will to play a distinctive part and to have one military role that was not that of the great powers. The bloom has gone off that role somewhat, and larger powers are now more involved in the operations. But for some time to come, Canadians are likely to regard this as something they can do well, and international bodies are still likely to look to them to contribute.

Historical Determinants

Canada's unique history also accounts for the nature of its foreign policies. Here one has to tread warily through glib deductions about the Canadian temperament, most of which have been overstated but have some validity.

On broad world issues, Canadians probably are more inclined than Americans to regard compromise as a good rather than a bad word. This trait has been traced to the fact that an ungainly country of two nations has of necessity lived on compromise, finding satisfaction in that it has had no revolution and no civil war. Canada has not fought, it has bargained its way to its present position of medium power and influence, although its contribution to the cause in two world wars legitimized its seat at the table. Living reasonably comfortably with contradictions comes more easily to Canadians than Americans, for they were premature détentists. Not having the power to contemplate banishing evil from the earth, they are less inclined to insist on unconditional surrender. They are pragmatists and functionalists, not messianic but smug. There has been a persistent scepticism about the use of economic sanctions, for example, not because punishment is undeserved but because sanctions rarely work. Canadian citizens often demand such gestures; their governments, more aware of the limitations on influence, remain sceptical. Canadians in government are canny crusaders. One most recognize, of course, that these traits may be attributable to the greater scope for objectivity of a country on the sidelines of critical issues. On broad world issues Canada rarely has to come up with an instant policy.

Canada grew up within a comfortable institution, the Empire-Commonwealth. It has benefited somewhat in twentieth-century diplomacy with a strong anti-colonialist bias from the fact that it was once a colony. There is something slightly fraudulent in the image, for Canada retained the colonial link for as long as it seemed in its interest to do so. It exploited the imperial power for its own purposes and took over control of its foreign policy only when it had to. On matters Canada considered important, like immigration and commerce, the decisions were made in Ottawa long before the formal right to do so was accorded. The British Foreign Office was expected to look after Canadian interests and pay the cost until Canada was ready to relieve them step by step. Among other advantages Canada was able to avoid the forced growth of a foreign service as suffered by many emergent countries and moved on to the world scene with an able group of men who acquired a reputation that has stood the country in good stead. Images, both good and bad, cling to a country long after they may be valid, especially in the case of a country with a pretty hazy *gestalt*.

Membership in the League of Nations gave Canada international status and a dubious reputation. The experience of error proved salutary. Shaping the UN was taken very seriously, so that Canadian governments retained for some time a kind of possessive attitude to the body. Canada, along with Australia and New Zealand, led the battle to limit the rule of the great powers and expand that of the lesser powers according to function. It recognized not so much the privileges as the obligations of the great powers, specifically in matters of security. A suspicion of commitment without a voice in policy is deep-rooted and accounts for a persistent reluctance to participate in regional or universal bodies in which Canada does not retain its right to decide whether or not to fight. It accounts also for a sensitivity about unilateralism on the part of the leading power, although Canada accepts the fact that the leader is not *comme les autres*. It is just one more paradox a lesser power has to live with.

NATO is another institution in the construction of which Canada played a significant role. Contrary to the views of American revisionists, NATO was, in the beginning, a kind of conspiracy by the British and Canadians to entrap the U.S. Senate into a commitment to Europe. It served Canada's need for collective defence, and on a multilateral rather than bilateral scale. A certain possessiveness about NATO also suffused Canadian policy makers for a long time, but the sense of responsibility has diminished somewhat, possibly because the alliance is increasingly regarded as a somewhat confrontational link between Europe and the United States.

Some of the older and larger powers regard international institutions as bodies that have inhibited their rights, but for Canadians they are places to establish a reputation, to gain their ends and in which to find space and an identity. In spite of disillusionment, the UN, NATO, and the Commonwealth are still perceived as associations that serve that purpose.

Canada's own slow development of a foreign policy and a foreign office strengthened its functionalist and organic approach to international institutions and its rejection of utopianism. Canadian governments have dedicated major resources to the cause of a universal law of the sea as a consolidation of consensus rather than as the imposition of a perfect scheme. That has always been the approach to the shaping of the UN, the Commonwealth and NATO. This priority for structures reflects also, of course, the vital need of a middle power for institutions in which it can act through coalitions, institutions that can lay down rules and regulations to protect it from the more powerful. In the case of the law of the sea, there is, along with the world order idealism, the vested interest of a country with an enormous coastline. Foreign critics say that Canada's unilateral action on Arctic waters in 1970 and protectionist measures like its Foreign Investment Review Agency (FIRA) in spite of GATT agreements do not indicate great deference to international institutions. These are arguable complaints ad hoc but it should be noted that Canada defended its pollution control zone in the Arctic as a means in desperation of moving the maritime powers to a revision of an antiquated law of the sea, an explanation that looks more valid in hindsight than it did at the time. As for GATT, the Canadian government does not believe it is acting contrary to the rules. What is important is that it did not contest the U.S. reference of FIRA to GATT, but called this the civilized way of handling a dispute. It has also favoured reference of the eastern maritime boundary to the international court.

Canada is still a developing country, though it takes its place in the Group of Seven industrialized powers. The ambiguity does affect its perspective on issues such as multinational corporations or the right to nationalization. In North-South negotiations it is a natural co-chairman. Since 1945 it has shared with the United States a coincidental interest in a freer world economy. Nevertheless, in the Forties it had also some fellow feeling for the European countries that could not afford free trade until they were on their feet, and now it understands out of its own experience the need of vulnerable economies for protection against 'global free enterprise'. Of course, this reputation for understanding the plight of the unfortunate puts considerable pressure on the country to make concessions and sacrifices itself and that is the perpetual rub.

Canada's mediatory diplomacy, which gave it a reputation in the postwar decades, involved the country's emotions, but not the substantive concerns of the electorate. The government did not doubt that it was pursuing the national interest because the maintenance of a favourable world order was regarded as the highest priority. But its high-wire diplomacy did not greatly affect the Canadian economy. Since then, the world has become more competitive and Canada more prosperous and more vulnerable. The electorate has become more aware of the international aspects of economic policy and its espousal of international regulation is tempered by a stronger concern for protection. The mood of the public, as in other countries in these straitened times, is narrower in its view of what is required. There is more scepticism about foreign aid. There is also greater caution about offending customers.

There always were conflicts between the short– and long–range national interest and the change is partly in terminology. Foreign policy was once thought of as grand diplomacy on the political and strategic level. Now the concept is more embracing. If one is to predict, it might be wisest to assume that economic calculations will carry even more weight than in the past, but that this will be attributable as much to the drastic state of the world as to departmental reorganization or changes in government. One hears much of a shift of priorities to economic foreign policy, but that always was the priority for Canada. It just wasn't previously called foreign policy and it did not fix Canada in the eyes of the world the way Lester B. Pearson did at the United Nations.

Tour d'Horizon

Generalizations about the foreign policy of a middling power with world-wide interests can be misleading. The agenda of Canada's foreign policy is long and varied, and although there is detectable a certain persistence of attitudes, there are manifold inconsistencies and that is a good thing. Our policies must be judged ad hoc. It would be folly to try in the time allowed to summarize briefly our attitudes to all parts of the globe and outer space. What follows is not a comprehensive survey of our policies and attitudes on important areas of foreign policy but a few observations on some of the more controversial issues.

The North

In the early postwar days, Canadians saw themselves as the Belgium of a new war. The fear of a nuclear exchange between the superpowers over Canadian air space, with devastating effects on those beneath, is still a note struck by Canadians in discussion of nuclear disarmament. It encourages a disposition to see the confrontation itself rather than just the Soviet Union as the threat to Canada. The conditioning of Canadians is such, however, that they do not equate the threat from the superpowers. It is not really a question of being on the U.S. side but of the U.S. being on their side.

The Canadian zeal in the cause of non-proliferation is attributable to a belief since 1945 in the essentiality of keeping to a minimum the number of nuclear powers. Canada was the first atomic power to renounce the military option on its own. This feeling has been strong enough to induce Conservative and Liberal governments to remove Canada's nuclear role in NATO and NORAD. Because this is done in the interests of non-proliferation rather than simple moral rejection of the bomb, it is regarded as not necessarily inconsistent with association in an alliance with a nuclear strategy. Canada's attitude to U.S. nuclear policy has never been one of outright opposition. Rather it has been marked by persistent fear of recklessness. When Canada has on occasion questioned American alert procedures under NORAD, it has been out of fear that such activity on the Arctic frontier would scare the Russians into regrettable conclusions. It is the Arctic, where Canada is vulnerable to Soviet strategic capabilities, that gives Canada some leverage on U.S. strategic arms policy.

Somewhat more subjective is the effect of 'Northernness' on the Canadian psyche and *Weltanschaung* — 'the true north strong and free'. All foreign policies have a certain romantic dimension, although as Canadian life has become softer, the Northern angst has been corrupted by the 'Florida sickness'. Canada's middle power diplomacy was developed in concert with Norway, Sweden, and Denmark at the UN and in NATO. There is an affinity with the Scandinavians, who share not only northern reaches but also similar political attitudes and institutions, from constitutional monarchy to a protestant guilt complex.

The racial problems of the North are likely to mean that Canada becomes more vulnerable to the kind of pressures in the UN that she has hitherto largely escaped as a reputedly non-imperialist power. In any case, the northern mystique remains a factor, not easily quantifiable, in the Canadian perspective of its place in the world. The Arctic is the one of its three ocean frontiers in which it is a major power — or at least a major presence.

The Pacific

The present demand for more activity in the Pacific is largely commercial and cultural. The Canadian attitude to Pacific security has been conditioned by the wartime experience. Canadian forces had been deployed on the European front for two years before Pearl Harbor and it made no sense to move them as a token to co-operation. After the war, Canadians were quite happy to leave the Pacific to the Americans. The Americans seemed to want it that way and there was really very little a lesser power could do. Nothing like a

North Pacific Treaty Organization was conceivable and without such a framework, a small ally could not find a satisfactory *modus vivendi* for participation. It was certainly not wanted in SEATO.

This is a point to be borne in mind when considering the role of the lesser members of NATO in conflict outside the NATO area. An alliance is attractive to them because it has a design for smaller powers, with stipulated autonomy and some right to a voice in policy. However much they might agree with their allies on action in the Middle East, for example, Canadians will be cautious about being the wagged tail in forces for the Sinai or the Persian Gulf. It is a particular difficulty of association in this way with the U.S. because Canadians know that, whatever agreements on policy they might reach with the U.S. administration, their task would be subjected to the vagaries of Congress. Formal joint policymaking is unfair for lesser powers and it would tie the hands of larger powers unacceptably.

The North Atlantic

The tendency of the Europeans to caucus in NATO and even at the UN has tended to isolate Canada in the alliance. In practice the alignments in NATO are not in the European-American confrontational pattern persistently and mischievously depicted by politicians and the media. Canada has strongly supported the Europeans over the Siberian pipeline and has been closer to the Germans and Dutch on sanctions and arms control. In fact the divisions in NATO, as seen from Ottawa, are more often between the superpower and the others and without geographical significance. Though there are issues on which Canada has a North American perspective and coincidental interests with the United States, just as often its perspectives are those of the lesser powers. With the persistent conviction, however, that trans-Atlantic good relations are the basis of Canadian security and its hopes of prosperity, there is always a strong disposition to try to heal any breaches.

North America

It is inevitable that bilateral conflict, competition and co-operation with the United States will condition Canadian foreign policy to the world at large. As superpowers go, the United States has been remarkably tolerant — or unobservant — of heresy in the north, if not the south. Nervousness by a

Canadian cabinet over Congressional response to Canadian actions on China or Cuba or Poland will induce caution, but American attitudes can also provoke stubbornness. The only generalization is that the relationship on this level is human, composed of resentments, expectations, irritations, gratitude, etc., unpredictable but important. Canadians know that divorce is impossible and that, for all its forbearance, or unawareness, the United States has the capacity (if it could ever get its act together) to crush Canada by non-military means. Therefore there are limits. The issue as to whether Canada can have an 'independent' foreign policy, which bothers some Canadians in the abstract seems to most an unreal issue, because of the unlikelihood of Canadians actually wanting to go beyond those limits. Within them there is plenty of room for divergence.

Canadian complaints are less about American 'leadership' than about its 'alliancemanship'. Most Canadians share the assumption that international relations in North America are on a higher moral level than those on other continents. They also fear that the consolidation of the European Community and other regional economic zones could leave Canada few alternatives to a closer economic continentalization, a prospect that, like most issues of the relationship, requires a calculation of profit and loss.

In its own policies vis-à-vis the rest of the world, Canada frequently has a variant approach from that of the United States which, within its power, it will advance, as tactfully as possible. Although it could not accept a veto or commit itself to any lopsided arrangement for determining common policies, it has been prepared in extremis to sacrifice on an ad hoc basis its own positions, rather than see the United States seriously weakened or suffer a critical loss of prestige. In this it does not differ greatly, because of proximity, from the other allies, except possibly that some of them, Britain for instance, have on the whole been more reluctant than Canada to differ from the United States. Canada, feeling somewhat more confident than they of the inevitability of American concern with its security, has risked more often American wrath. Canada does, of course, take advantage of the fact that Americans notice what the British and French do, but Canada can withdraw half its troops from Europe without Congress paying much attention.

Latin America and the Caribbean

On one area of the world the Canadian line of sight differs markedly from that of the United States. That is Latin America, which Canadians cannot see very well beyond the U.S. The Western Hemisphere is not so much a geographical as a historical phenomenon, linking the United States and the Latin countries. The Bolivar connection was never part of Canadian history and Canada was the accepted anomaly in the Monroe Doctrine. In the flush of enthusiasm for international institutions after the war, Canada favoured universal bodies, partly because it did not want America and Europe divided again, partly because it did not like the regions in which it might be cast. In specialized agencies it had more in common with Western Europe and the Rio Treaty was a commitment in an area beyond what Canadians considered their region of special concern.

As for Central America in general, Canada has remained aloof, though the public gets steamed up over issues that become controversial elsewhere, such as El Salvador. For years Canadian governments have had a differing perspective from Washington on the link between revolutionary movements and Moscow. That has rarely meant flat opposition to the United States, but doubts about ways and means and interpretations — not to mention the information from U.S. intelligence sources. An awareness of the awful contradictions on the ground and a certain reticence about public preaching would prevent Ottawa from flatly opposing U.S. actions in El Salvador or Nicaragua, but it will also be reticent about categorical support. With a few exceptions Canada has adhered to the British traditional attitude to diplomatic relations as a matter of convenience, not an indication of affection. It was for this reason, and a fear of driving Castro to the Russians, that a Canadian Conservative government did not sever trade or diplomatic relations with Cuba in 1959. No succeeding government has ever publicly considered changing that policy.

The Commonwealth and La Francophonie

It would be a mistake to regard Canada's zeal in the Commonwealth as anti-American, because it is a conviction in Ottawa that this informal association, where representatives of North and South can talk to each other with unusual frankness and mutual comprehension, serves the interests of the United States — though it is probably the only international organization except the Warsaw pact to which no American official ever pays tribute. At the same time an undoubted attraction is that it is an association in which Canada is a large fish and the superpower is not an overwhelming presence. In the company it keeps, Canada does have a hankering after space in which to breathe and the Commonwealth provides it. It is in no sense an exclusive attachment. Canadians find a certain measure of freedom in belonging to a variety of associations. That is part of the functionalist perspective. The international francophone connection provides another outlet, although it has as yet not become a consultative body like the Commonwealth.

Cultural Policy

The sense of being Canadian has grown with a common history, but Canada is not and never will be a national state on the European model or a missionary state like the U.S.A. It is in fact something more modern, a framework of convenience, the stated aim of which is 'peace, order and good government'. In this way it is a more interesting model for the new countries of Africa — a fact which is in the minds of Canadians devising a foreign policy towards that continent.

Battered as they are (and also stimulated) by the culture of larger countries of different species, Canadians too often lose confidence in their own individuality and worry excessively and tiresomely about their identity. (This irritates foreigners who think they can always identify a Canadian by the large bundle of chips he carries on his shoulder.) Foreigners are often inclined to think that this glorification of looseness is nothing but a rationalization of failure, but the functionalist Canadian response would be that a healthy ideal for a country must be derived from what geography and history have made it. The creation of a tightly-knit nation state out of Canada would be bound to fail. Canadians must therefore find success in what they are.

A problem of all smaller countries is the metropolitanization of culture and the consequent necessity to struggle against practical considerations to keep the arts healthy at home and the artists also at home where they can provide nourishment. The cultural product in Canada was never more abundant. That is not the problem. Canadians will go on reading Tolstoy and Flaubert or Saul Bellow, but they need in addition to have a literature about themselves and their own distinctive ways to understand themselves better. It irks Canadians, open to the cultures of the world, to be accused of cultural nationalism, not to speak of being called book-burners by a member of the American cabinet. As Northrop Frye has said: "Scholarship knows no boundaries. Scholarship may not, but culture does. The study of Canadian literature is not a painful patriotic duty like voting, but a simple necessity of getting one's bearings."

Nourishing the arts at home could not in such a loose and modern country be achieved by erecting a Berlin wall. It does require, however, some government action against centripetal forces, against publishers and film distributors who want to fit Canada into North American regions. Thanks to satellites and other forms of technology this is a universal problem of high order and larger countries than Canada are becoming worried. A writer for *le Monde* speculated that one day a Frenchman would have to consult a data bank in Washington to find out what happened on July 14, 1789.

Conclusion

There is a defensive character to Canadian foreign policy that is to some extent required by circumstances, but it leads to a few lamentable characteristics, in particular what Margaret Atwood has called the "myth of victimization". On the part of the public, although less so of officials, there is a tendency to regard independence as an end in itself and to take a scholastic view of influence. Given the fact that in its period of growth Canadians took a very sensible and functionalist view of independence as counterproductive for that time, it is curious that it has been such a preoccupation of many articulate debaters in recent years. A myth has grown up that control of foreign policy had to be wrested from the British. Then it was necessary to prove to the world after 1918 that Canada was a sovereign player on the world scene. It was assumed by some nationalists in earlier years that the only way Canada could prove that it was in charge of foreign policy was to differ from Britain. The government, however, showed that Canada could of its own will separately declare war alongside Britain and France — and Poland. After the war there was perpetuated a silly debate over whether Canada would follow the U.S. or Britain and there is some element of this old controversy still, in spite of the insistence of governments that Canada reaches its own conclusions. The challenge then appeared as one of proving that Canadian foreign policy was not made in Washington. Again the government proved that Canada could of its own will and with a great deal of its own initiative help concoct an alliance in which the United States would be one of the partners, and that it would nevertheless express its own views and pursue its own tactics in world affairs. Still, on many issues from El Salvador to Poland, policy debates are skewed by this false interpretation of independence as something that can be displayed on in divergence.

Whereas American influence on policies in this or other institutions is detailed daily in the media of the world and usually exaggerated, Canadian attitudes, whether expressed quietly or out loud, are rarely reported. The Canadian public has only a hazy idea of what its representatives are up to. They are better aware, therefore, of the vagaries of American foreign policy than their own and too apt irresponsibly to think that agreeing or disagreeing with the United States is all that Canadian foreign policy amounts to. There is what in the eyes of foreigners may often seem like an overestimate of Canadian input in official Canadian statements and an unrealistic demand from the Canadian public for more public displays of influence and independence.

It is not the grand themes that make up the major part of the agenda in the Canadian Department of External Affairs. It is not that Canadians have a different estimate of what is important to international relations. They know that the fate of Lebanon, strategic arms limitation and the confrontation between China and Vietnam are as important as the greater powers think they are. They do not intend to keep silent on these subjects. They must vote in the General Assembly and from time to time act with a great sense of responsibility in the Security Council. They take positions and try to mould opinion in the associations to which they belong. Nevertheless, they know that their role in these issues is usually peripheral. What they think about El Salvador or Kampuchea will not matter critically. Necessity dictates, therefore, that their attention be on issues that affect them more directly. Perhaps the concern about ownership of energy resources or the protection of Canadian television seem parochial in the eyes of those who focus on the grand strategies. They may be matters of survival to the lesser power. The survival of mankind is clearly of much greater importance, even in the eyes of Canadians concerned for the integrity of their national life. In their functionalist view, however, it is the greatest powers which largely determine the greatest issues and the preoccupation of the others, particularly those in relative security, are inevitably on smaller scale. However, the Canadian attitude to the role of a middle power has grown more sophisticated. It is seen functionally. A country is not small, middle or large across the board. A country that is a minor military power and a major-minor or minor-major economic power is going to concentrate on economic issues or territorial issues that matter to it and in which it matters. In spite of some spectacular ventures in grand diplomacy, that is where the foreign policy of Canada has always had its main thrust. That is also where it has considerable clout.

Colin Robertson

Born in Winnipeg and educated at the University of Manitoba and the Norman Paterson School of International Affairs at Carleton, Colin Robertson has served as a diplomat and Canadian Consul for more than twenty-five years. His postings have included five years in Hong Kong and several stints in the United States, including assignments in New York and Washington as well as four years as Consul General in Los Angeles.

Returning to Ottawa between international postings, he served as Director General of Public Affairs for Treasury Board and Director General of Communications for the Department of Foreign Affairs. He is currently Minister (Advocacy) and Head of the Washington Secretariat at the Canadian Embassy.

Married to journalist and public relations specialist Maureen Boyd, Colin has three well-travelled children and an amiable golden retriever.

This paper was first given as the 1997 Queen-Hughes Lecture.

The 1997 Queen-Hughes Lecture

Slouching Toward The Millennium: Can Canada Make a Difference?

by Colin Robertson

EVELYN WAUGH wrote that we are what we are because of where we came from: at the end of the day memories are made of the people and places that matter to us.

If he was right, tonight I am surrounded by what I am: my parents, my favourite aunt and uncle, my old professor, who steered me to a career in foreign affairs, friends from my school days, the institute itself — I joined the CIIA as a student twenty-three years ago. Wilf Queen-Hughes, in whose name this lecture is given, had recently died and I have no doubt that one of the first lectures I attended was one given in his honour.

Jan Morris, that chronicler of Empire and author of place and people, has not included Winnipeg in her accounts. If she had, I am convinced that she would pronounce it as a place and people with a broader sense of the world. One of my earliest memories was attending Travelogues in the old Playhouse theatre with my Grandmother Cruden, where I would often fall asleep — but not before I had a glimpse of far-away places and people.

I remember going with my Grandmother Robertson to the *Winnipeg Free Press* for Stamp Club, where we would trade those little bits of paper from far away places with romantic names like Tanganyika and Zanzibar. They had pictures of people like Zog of Yugoslavia. Most came from the dominions and colonies ruled by Victoria, Edward VII or one of the Georges. It was a world coloured rose red and so depicted in a famous two-penny stamp issued by Canada a century ago to mark the Jubilee.

How the world has changed! For much of my lifetime 'red' signified something quite else — Communism. For my grandchildren, I hope that Communism will have the same curio effect as the two-penny red.

The Free Press, where we held our stamp meetings, is intimately connected, of course, with the CIIA. Its great editor, John Dafoe, was one of the creators of the institute.

Canada may have come of age on places like Vimy Ridge and Yypres, but it was a coming of age with a huge cost. Two of my Grandmother Robertson's brothers died on those far-away fields, a third came back with what we would now describe as post-traumatic stress disorder, but was then known as shell shock. To ensure it really was the war to end all wars, Dafoe argued for collective security and for putting in place organizations like the Canadian Institute of International Affairs, which would educate the common man and woman about the wider world. Dafoe was a great democrat and he had more faith in the common sense of the average citizen than in the aristocratic elite of Europe.

There was a sense that the wider world mattered, that for a country like Canada independence went hand-in-hand with collective security. Ours was not, to use the memorable phrase of Senator Raoul Dandurand, "a fire-proof house far from inflammable material". It is that sense — that the wider world matters to us — that I wish to address tonight.

The title of my talk, 'Slouching Towards the Millennium: Can Canada make a Difference?', draws its inspiration from one of my favourite poems, 'The Second Coming', by William Butler Yeats.

You will recognize the opening lines:

> Things fall apart, the centre cannot hold;
> Mere anarchy is loosed upon the world,
> The best lack all conviction, while the worst
> Are full of passionate intensity.

It concludes:

> And what rough beast, its hour come round at last,
> Slouches towards Bethlehem to be born?

Yeats wrote of the world in the aftermath of the Great War. I think the beast of which he writes included the four horsemen of the apocalypse: Famine, Disease, War and Slaughter. As we look around the world today one could say that not much has changed. Famine continues to be a part of life for much of the world.

And disease — AIDS wreaks havoc in much of Central Africa as well as in Southeast Asia. Tuberculosis, malaria, typhoid — those diseases that we thought we had beaten with the wonder drug of our century, penicillin – are making a comeback.

Violence, in what my American foreign service colleagues described as 'pygmy wars', continues to be a way of life in Africa and Asia. The slaughter of innocents continues to strike close to home — terrorism has become a fact of life in most of the major capitals of the world. We should not take our own immunity lightly.

As we close this century, verdicts are being passed. Isaiah Berlin, the British philosopher and maker of that splendid phrase "the crooked timber of humanity" calls it the "most terrible century in Western history".

Yehudi Menuhin, whose music must rank as one of the greatest gifts of this century, says that "it raised the greatest hopes ever conceived by humanity, and destroyed all illusions and ideals".

For our part, we privileged few in the West live longer and better than ever. We are the best-educated generation in the history of mankind. Through the progress of science and technology we have put men on the moon and explored both our planet and our universe. Our knowledge of life has expanded a hundredfold.

And we live in a world of constant change. At the beginning of this century most Canadians lived in small towns or on farms. Farming was the main occupation. During the next forty years there was a great migration to the cities and by mid-century most of us lived in places like Winnipeg. My grandfathers were employed in two of the great industries: Ogilvy Flour Mills and Swifts. They were jobs for life, jobs with a future. Swifts shut down nearly twenty years ago and Ogilvy Flour has long since closed.

To assure ourselves of a job today, we look to the post-industrial tools of high technology. Computers, once kept behind lock and key for use by the military and technological elite, are now the playthings of our children. Today I carry in my watch and portable computer more memory and capacity than was possessed by the Allies at the end of the Second World War. Arthur Schlesinger has calculated that this century — roughly two lifetimes, has seen more change than the planet's first 798 lifetimes put together.

The question is twofold: Can we deal with change? And, in this change, can Canada make a difference?

My response is: Yes, we can manage change. And yes, Canada can continue to make a difference. In this century, the great issues of our time have been those of war and peace and the efforts to achieve a measure of security. The democracies were pitted first against autocracy, then fascism and finally communism. In each case, at immense cost in blood and treasure, the side of democracy has triumphed.

Why? Because freedom matters.

I am convinced by all that I have observed throughout my foreign service career that at the end of the day, the human instinct for freedom ultimately triumphs.

And it is in the quest for freedom and the establishment of the rule of law, on which freedom must rest, that Canada can make a difference. For Canada is, more by chance than design, a microcosm of the global village. We have within our borders the peoples of all nations. Unlike most of the rest of the world, we distinguish ourselves not by class, nor creed nor colour. Anyone can come to this country and become not just a citizen, but prime minister or premier. And we accomplish this not through the bullet, but by the ballot The number of countries around the world that feature this kind of equality of opportunity and access can be counted on the fingers of one hand.

Let me make two sets of observations on the international landscape. The first is how through the pursuit of three twentieth-century concepts we have preserved the peace in our time. These concepts are first, collective security; second, generosity to the defeated and poor, and third, the key role of multilateralism.

The second set of observations will describe three challenges for the future: first, the impact of globalization on our economy; second, the need to link policy to respect for our environment, and third, the effect of movements of people.

Preserving Peace In Our Time
Collective Security Works

My first observation: the system of collective security, originally advocated by people like John Dafoe and designed by Canadians like Mike Pearson and Escott Reid, has worked extraordinarily well. Designed, as Pug Ismay, the first Secretary General of NATO put it, "to keep the Russians out, the Americans in and the Germans down", the Western alliance, of which NATO is the centerpiece, has kept the peace for half a century. This is no small accomplishment.

The last time a comparable grand alliance was created in peacetime was in 1815, after Waterloo, when Britain, Austria, Prussia and Russia formed the quadruple alliance to keep Napoleon and his family off the throne of France and to defend the territorial settlement of the Congress of Vienna. That alliance lasted seven years.

An aside: Next year [1998] NATO will be expanded to include Poland, the Czech Republic and Hungary. We know this angers and upsets the Russians. Their first response was to say that it would delay indefinitely any favourable consideration by the Russian parliament of the Start II treaty, which had been counted on to slash the number of nuclear weapons in Russian and U.S. missile silos. There is also the question of how the U.S. and its allies, including Canada, will stretch a shrinking military force to protect Warsaw, Prague and Budapest.

Magnanimous in Victory

A second observation: Western generosity, particularly that of the United States toward Germany and Japan, after the peace settlement of 1945, has had a profoundly positive effect. We put in practise the most difficult part of Churchill's dictum: "In war, resolution; in defeat, defiance; in victory, magnanimity; in peace, goodwill."

It is a remarkable feature of American leadership over the past half century that the U.S. enthusiastically financed and supported the progress of Western Europe and Japan to become economic powers. The character of Germany and Japan has changed. Neither Japan nor Germany have sought to use their economic strength to become the military power that their wealth would permit. This is a huge and important change.

Between 1864 and 1939, Germany launched five wars. For diplomats after Metternich there has been one abiding issue: the German Question. Yet anyone who has watched Germany in my lifetime can only conclude that Germans have genuinely repudiated authoritarian government. They are also successfully integrating the people of what was formerly the German Democratic Republic into the new Germany. This continues to be no small challenge. But it is working.

Multilateralism Works

My third observation: we should not underestimate the extraordinary contribution of multilateral institutions in improving the well-being of humanity.

The United Nations is the centerpiece, but the groupings must also include institutions like the Commonwealth and Francophonie.

It is easy to dismiss the UN as wasteful and lethargic. And if you look only at the bureaucracy in New York or Paris, you would be right. But to appreciate the value of the UN you need to look beyond the bureaucracy. Look at its work in the field in terms of combating poverty, hunger and disease. I speak particularly of organizations like UNICEF in its work with children, the World Health Organization in Asia, Africa and Latin America, and the United Nations High Commission for Refugees.

The social and economic agencies play a role analogous to diplomats — you rarely hear of their work, because it is designed to prevent problems before they occur. Who can say how many conflicts have been prevented through the Colombo Plan or through the unsung volunteers in agencies like CUSO, World University Overseas and the Ottawa-based IDRC? The latter is the model par excellence for international development agencies. And keep in mind that the monies spent supporting the multilateral system is less than five per cent of what the world spends on arms each year. There is no question as to which is the better value.

Looking Ahead

Now let me look to the future ... we have a unique status as the greatest of the middle powers, hovering somewhere between the arrogance of the great powers and impotence of the small. And we are without doubt the greatest of the middle powers; we pull more than our weight in the councils of state. Nonetheless, I think that we sometimes try to be all things to all people. Increasingly, we will have to be more selective in our internationalism.

If politics and security dominated international affairs in this century, in the next century, I believe the great challenges will fall under three headings: the Global Economy, the Environment and the Movements of People.

The Global Economy
Trade matters more than ever before, especially to Canada. Our economic recovery has been driven by our trade, especially with the United States. Markets have always mattered to Canada; they matter even more today.

I spent almost half of my professional career working on trade policy, first in preparations for the negotiations, which later resulted in the Free Trade Agreement of 1988, and five years later in the negotiations that resulted in the North American Free Trade Agreement. Trade matters.

The competition comes from the economic superpowers: the United States, Japan, Germany and its partners in the European Community, as well as new players like South Korea, Taiwan, Brazil and Mexico. The growth along the old 'gold coast' of China promises the creation of a hundred Hong Kongs. India has the largest middle class in the world and it will use its engineers and software specialists to join the high–tech world.

If the United Nations defined multilateralism for the past fifty years then for the next half-century the center of attention will be the World Trade Organization. Diplomats of my generation vie not for assignments to the New York and the UN but rather in Geneva and the WTO. In Europe, North Asia and the Americas the agenda is dominated not by issues of political boundaries but economic integration.

It is not always recognized that our own niche in the international ecosystem is in economic rather than security multilateralism. We gain greater leverage through our membership in the G–7, OECD, WTO and Quadrilateral Meetings of Trade Ministers. The defining foreign policy moment of the first Chrétien government must surely be 'Team Canada' and its emphasis on economics and Asia. And 1997 is the Year of Asia.

Here I think the choices for Canada are both easy and obvious. The wealth we create through trade pays the bills. We must continue to seek free and open markets. We will do this in multilateral organizations like the WTO and APEC as well as in bilateral and regional settings, like what we have achieved through the FTA, then NAFTA and now through free trade agreements with countries like Chile and Israel.

And trade is like the proverbial loaves and fishes. The economic pie, as Adam Smith observed nearly two hundred years ago, just keeps getting bigger. Everyone wins.

I would also argue, as John Dafoe did in 1911, that opening borders to trade promotes democracy. Rising incomes go hand in hand with higher standards in education and health care and the development of representational government.

There is considerable debate today about an 'inevitable clash of civilizations' between Islam and the West. The rise of ethnicity also gets thrown into this debate. As trade borders are erased, paradoxically, national identity becomes more important. But just as we exchange some of our sovereignty by becoming economically independent, we seek a stronger cultural identity. Our roots, our nationalities become more important. This presents obvious challenges.

As for the rise of Islamic fundamentalism: the truth is that Islamic movements are driven more by appalling local social conditions than by ideology. The core issues in the Islamic world are primarily economic: the widening gap between rich and poor, inflation, unemployment, massive corruption and disillusionment with the ruling elite. I believe that trade and targeted application of development assistance will effect greater positive change than preparing for a new Crusade.

There is considerable debate about the efficiency of development assistance. I am convinced it works, but we need to return to the basic purpose as it was described by Pearson around the Colombo Plan: aim to improve quality of life by training middle and lower grade workers and technicians in the areas in which they live. And increasingly we should see ourselves as 'facilitators' rather than solely as 'doers'. Recently, for example, CIDA, drawing on its thirty years of experience, has undertaken the delivery of Japanese development projects in Africa. Japan provides the money, we provide the on-site expertise. It was a concept practised by the Americans during Desert Storm, when Japan and Germany bankrolled the American military machine. Frankly, if we, too, are to be mercenaries because of money problems, let us be development mercenaries.

To have a budget for development assistance you need public support at home. Public support is much easier to generate when there are not beggars in the street, nor are your Mom or Dad or brother and sister without jobs. In short, the prerequisite is a healthy economy at home.

Canada must continue to carve out its niche and develop a catalogue of specialty goods and services. In developing our own vast country we have achieved competitive advantage in areas like telecommunications and transportation engineering. Canadian firms like Northern Telecom are wiring the telephone systems in places like Peking and Buenos Aires. Bombardier is building the subway system in New York and Bangkok. Today, communications and telecommunications employ more Canadians than mining and petroleum combined. More Canadians work in our electronics industry than in pulp and paper. The computer industry now employs more than the entire air transport system.

We have inherent advantages. The rule of law governs business. We have an educated workforce. And we have our natural resources, the driving force for our economy during our first century. But natural resources no longer drive economic growth. The emphasis today is on knowledge. Biotechnology is transforming medicine, agriculture, food and chemicals as well as our resource industries: forestry, fisheries and mining.

In 1991, Michael Porter of Harvard's Business School conducted a survey on behalf of the government and the Business Council on National Issues. Calling it 'Canada at the Crossroads: The Reality of a New Competitive Environment', the conclusion bears repeating: The nature of competition between nations is undergoing radical change and what made us rich in the past does not necessarily hold true for the future. In tomorrow's world, wealth will be created, not inherited. For Canada, it means trade and creating, through education, a work-force with the skills to compete.

It will require unprecedented cooperation between governments: federal, provincial and municipal. It will require, for example, setting aside squabbles on constitutional responsibility for education. It will require a real commitment to reducing interprovincial trade barriers.

The challenge is not only for government, but for business and educators as well. How do we best equip ourselves so that we can maintain our standard of living? Are our schools teaching what we need to know for the next century? Where do governments put their increasingly strained resources? Is it better to subsidize a firm that promises to create employment for today or a Centre for Biotechnology that will create the jobs of tomorrow?

The Environment
Increasingly, we are finding economic development can only be sustained in the long run by respecting our environment. Any gardener or farmer will tell you if you overfertilize or fail to respect nature's natural regeneration you bring yourself disaster. What holds true for our gardens holds true for the global commons.

Building higher smokestacks to drive away the pollution caused by burning coal in Pittsburgh only served to sterilize the lakes of Eastern Canada. Visit Bangkok or Shenzhen or the maquiladoras on the border between the U.S. and Mexico and within minutes you will begin choking on the results of mindless industrialization.

Both natural evolution and human social development have been shaped by our ecology. Each year the world adds eighty-seven million more people — more than the entire population of Germany. Chronic water shortages now plague more than eighty countries, home to forty per cent of the world's population. The demand for food continues to push against production capacity. Weather extremes have reduced harvests in the great bread–baskets of China, the United States and Canada twice in this decade.

It is not just agriculture that is vulnerable to climate change. So are our fishing industry, forest products and insurance. I make special reference to insurance because insurance is increasingly linked to our financial services. It is from this quarter that pressure will ultimately come to make meaningful change. The global insurance industry paid out $57 billion in weather-related claims between 1990 and 1995, compared to $17 billion during the 1980s.

Global warming is the main cause of climate change, but there are other threats to our ecology: radioactive waste, ozone depletion, acid rain, pesticides. For the past half-century our greatest fear was annihilation by nuclear bomb. Today there is a new clock reading five minutes to midnight. As the Club of Rome warned, it is the threat to human survival coming from ecological destruction through misuse of Mother Earth.

And let us not forget the connection between environment and disease. With global warming and population growth, the new millennium will be an unalloyed boon for parasites. Mosquitoes will live longer and bite harder. Man's changing habitat will promote the appearance of new diseases, so that Legionnaire's disease, Ebola, Lassa, Marburg, Hanta viruses, and AIDS will seem like mere 'curtain raisers'.

All this is forcing a re-examination of how we live. It will mean more than putting the papers and tins in the blue box. It is going to require every decision to be referenced against an environmental assessment. Environment departments will become as much a central agency of government as the Finance or Foreign Policy portfolio. This will not come easily, especially in the developing world which views the West's environmental concerns as sanctimony at best, at worst, a latent form of protectionism designed to curb their economic development.

The Movement of Peoples
As never before, the peoples of the world are on the move. The United Nations High Commissioner for Refugees reckons the number of people throughout the world that are displaced by war, famine and disease is approximately thirty million — roughly the population of Canada.

According to the International Labour Organization the total workforce of the Third World will be 600 to 700 million people larger by the millennium than it was in 1980. To employ all these additional workers, developing countries will have to create more jobs than now exist in Japan, the European Union and the United States combined.

Obviously, this will not happen and many of those who cannot find work will decide to leave. From watching American crime shows, we know the pressure now put on the southern border of the United States by migrants from Mexico and Central America. Population growth in Latin America has been exceptionally fast. The combined population of Latin American countries was about 150 million during the 1950s. It is expected to be 845 million by 2025. Half of the people in Latin America are eighteen years old and they are looking for work. How will we respond? This will be a particular pressure point for Canada because of our relatively open borders.

The Americans have responded with a blend of policies. NAFTA was partly driven by American policy makers' sense that creating economic growth, which worked for Western Europe after the war, was a better solution than creating along their southern border the sort of wall that previously defined the boundaries between East and West Berlin.

Nonetheless, they have done just that — built a wall along parts of their frontier between Texas, California and Mexico. Weeks ago, Congress passed and the president signed the most restrictive refugee control measures since the Second World War. Immigration control is the one part of their budget on which there was all-party agreement to increase funding — mostly for border guards and equipment to keep out illegal migrants. Smuggling human beings is already as lucrative as smuggling drugs and weapons.

Nor are the Americans alone. Italian intervention in Albania has been prompted in part by a desire to keep Albanians out of Italy. In France, the electoral success of Monsieur LePen and his followers have resulted in governments of both the left and right cracking down on rights and refugees.

The movement of peoples raises a series of hard questions for democratic governments and their citizens. For example: How far can you go with police checks without infringing the rights of your citizens? Do you force everyone to start carrying ID cards? What happens to civil liberties? How far do we go in supporting multiculturalism? Do we spend money on English as a second language in our schools or insist that all immigrants learn it on their own?

What would we do, for example, if things went badly in Hong Kong and we were faced with a flood of between a half-million and 1.2 million Chinese from Hong Kong who, under the principles set by the UNHCR, would look to Canada as a home for resettlement?

Can Canada Make a Difference?

If we are slouching towards the millennium, can Canada Make a Difference? Yes. We can. In my travels throughout the world I concluded that Laurier was right: the twentieth century did indeed belong to Canada, not in the sense that we have traditionally defined greatness — military might and economic prowess — but in terms of what we have become as a nation. There is extraordinary envy and interest globally in how we have made Canada work.

Pearson observed a quarter-century ago in one of his final speeches as prime minister, that Canada is a model for international cooperation. Look around a classroom or your workplace. You will likely find peoples originally from all parts of the world. And it works. Foreign observers continually marvel at what we have achieved. We remain the most favoured state for potential immigrants. Our stability and peaceful society are greatly coveted. Baywatch may be more popular than the Beachcombers but 'Peace order and good government' beats out 'life, liberty and the pursuit of happiness'. The United Nations Development index continually puts Canada at the top of its list as the best country in the world in which to live.

I sometimes think that as a country we are a bit like George Bailey, the character played by Jimmy Stewart in *It's a Wonderful Life*. As you will recall, this is Frank Capra's film about a good man who is so busy helping others that life seems to pass him by and he wonders whether it would have been better that he had not been born.

As a country we perhaps suffer from a lack of confidence; it's the natural reaction of the self-described mouse living next to the elephant. But, like George, we do not realize how much we have done and how much we are admired abroad. The world would have been a poorer place without Canada. We have consistently punched beyond our weight.

We played a key and sustaining role in building and maintaining the institutions that have preserved the peace in our time and improved the living conditions of millions. We invented the role of middle power and defined 'functional responsibility' in international affairs. Its motto "Let those who can, do" prevented the great powers from disposing of our affairs to suit their convenience. As St. Laurent put it, the 'supermen' had had their day in the sun.

And we did a lot. Peacekeeping was a Canadian innovation. For years, we set the standard for international development assistance. We are forging a new niche for ourselves in 'peacebuilding', through the monitoring of free and fair elections — the prerequisite of democracy. And we are liked and admired around the world.

As we slouch towards the millennium, we can and we do make a difference.

Slouching Toward The Millennium: Can Canada Make a Difference?

DARYL COPELAND

Daryl Copeland is a Canadian Foreign Service officer who has served abroad in Thailand, Ethiopia, New Zealand and Malaysia. He was educated at the University of Western Ontario and Carleton University and has written and spoken widely on issues of foreign policy, political economy, diplomatic management, globalization and Canada's relations with the Asia Pacific Region.

At the Department of Foreign Affairs and International Trade in Ottawa, he has worked in nuclear energy policy, consular planning, and as senior intelligence analyst covering South/Southeast Asia and Japan. His most recent appointments have been as Deputy Director for International Communications, Director for Southeast Asia and Senior Advisor, Public Diplomacy. On secondment to the Canadian Institute of International Affairs in the late 1990s, he served as national programme director and editor of *Behind the Headlines*, Canada's international affairs magazine.

Elected to five terms on the Executive Committee of the Professional Association of Foreign Service Officers, he is now Foreign Affairs Canada and International Trade Canada representative to the Association of Professional Executives of the Public Service of Canada. In June 2000, he received the Canadian Foreign Service Officer Award for his "tireless dedication and unyielding commitment" to advancing the interests of the diplomatic profession.

Daryl is currently Director of Communications Services, responsible for publishing, editing, design, advertising and public opinion research.

He enjoys the arts, music, literature, photography, sports and, especially, travel and the outdoors.

This paper was first given as the 1998 Queen-Hughes Lecture.

The 1998 Queen-Hughes Lecture

Globalization and the National Prospect

by Daryl Copeland

GOING …

GLOBALIZATION IS ABOUT BORDERLESS NATIONS. Stateless firms. Infirm states. And a new frontier — without frontiers. That's the *Reader's Digest* version, anyway. Catchy, but hackneyed. Popular, but fuzzy.

So, what do Canadians really need to know about globalization? In truth, lots, because in terms of population, we are the world. We are also among the most trade and investment dependent countries on earth.

Let's start with principles and a definition. Globalization is a process in which a critical range of activities — economic, social and political — are transferred to world scale. Though this trend has been developing over decades, it has only recently taken a quantum leap in force and extent. And perhaps more than anything else, it is the striking speed with which globalization is occurring and the volatility and instability that have ensued, which together have generated such enormous challenges.

To date, and quite understandably, the negative aspects, referred to by Canada's former minister of Foreign Affairs, Lloyd Axworthy, as the "underside of globalization", have dominated the debate. The process of globalization is, however, two-sided, and thus generates opportunities and openings for creative responses even as it exacts certain costs. Though I will not dwell on it here, this point has been lost in much of the commentary.

So … Globalization creates wealth — and, I might add, takes it away, as British Columbia is learning in the wake of the economic turmoil in Asia. Globalization fosters dynamic efficiencies. It forces new economies of production. It makes national economies — or, at least, what's left of them — more internationally competitive. And it all comes at some cost — widening disparities, difficult adjustments, diminishing diversity, the erosion of civil society. Whatever else might be attributed, globalization has emerged as a defining historical phenomenon of our times, transforming structures and conditioning outcomes across a huge range of human activity.

So much for an introduction; it is time to enquire more deeply. At the most fundamental level, globalization has been driven by changes in the world economy, including: greater economic interdependence and technological capacity; increased mobility of finance and investment capital, and indeed of most factors of production (except labour), and higher levels of market integration and policy liberalization.

But globalization also has some preconditions. It could not be sweeping the world were it not for the revolutionary technological change witnessed in recent decades, first in transportation and communications, then in electronics, semiconductors, computers, and software. Advances in information technology, reduced costs, extensive databases, fibre-optic transmission, and interconnections between networks — the Internet foremost among them — have combined to compress both time and space. You can run, but you can't hide ... and the whole wired world's watching.

Though driven by a preoccupation with maximizing returns, globalization relies upon a complex of political institutions and conditions, including regional integration (NAFTA, APEC, EU, etc.), international trade negotiations (WTO, MAI), and the continuing conviviality of multilateral organizations. While United Nations Security Council muscle will still be required, on occasion, to compel the uncooperative, the real action will increasingly be in the World Trade Organization rather than the General Assembly.

In this new dispensation, world wars are out; world markets, world sourcing and world product mandates are in. The great game is over and the evil empire vanquished. Geopolitics has given way to geoeconomics.

... going ...

While globalization will one way or another affect virtually everyone and everything, corporations have been best placed to reap the benefits. It is states that face particularly tough times. In capitals around the world, governments seem too big to do the small things, and too small to do the big things. Hollowed out by ethnic and regional uprisings from within, eroded top to bottom by demands for decentralization, and buffeted on all sides by uncontrollable forces, national governance has perhaps never been more difficult. Though by no means cause for universal regret, the changing nature of the state in the face of globalization certainly merits a closer look.

The articulation of national policies and values, the pursuit of national interests, the collection and redistribution of national wealth, and the administration of national economic space has, for most of the twentieth century, been a central part of what states do. Yet compliance with the provisions of trade agreements has for many states translated into significant intrusions, with broad implications for domestic management and national identity.

In particular, the maximization of efficiency in a global economy requires an unprecedented degree of policy uniformity, which in turn involves a substantial surrender of national decision-making control. Some, such as Sylvia Ostry, call these systems friction, others, like Maude Barlow, see a new imperialism. Whatever your preference, the impact of globalization on sovereignty, popular and national, is enormous.

… going …
Throughout the world, many of the traditional tenets that have informed public policy and administration are under siege. The ethic of universal and equitable access to services is giving way to that of contracting out, cost recovery, and user payment.

That this has occurred at the same time as service reductions, regulatory rollbacks, and a transfer of the burden of taxation from companies to wage earners, has led some analysts to conclude that globalization is tantamount to the imposition of some kind of corporate agenda, the accumulation of private power, at the expense of the public interest, under the guise of an attack on government.

Wherever one comes out on that issue, it is clear that many policy areas that were once the exclusive preserve of national governments have been internationalized, privatized or simply abandoned. The orientation of the state is changing and its capabilities are diminishing rapidly as transnational linkages, economic integration and interdependence combine to weaken both the fiscal positions of national governments and their independence.

As for the apparatus of the state, large swathes of its regulatory, administrative and program delivery capacity have already been dismantled or sold off. Public services, utilities and parks are being repackaged as business opportunities and corporatized.

… gone …

This withering of the legitimacy and domain of state activity appears to have produced both a degree of policy paralysis and a recalibration of the popular vision of government. Within the elites, the old, benign image of the state as the embodiment of shared values, arbiter of competing demands, and agent of distributive justice has to a significant extent been eclipsed by the triumph of pro-business, anti-public sector values. The Ronald Reagan, Paul Martin, Mike Harris model of anti-government government is clearly ascendant.

The welfare vocation — which had always been predicated on a degree of national protection and the isolation of certain services from market forces — has given way to the new imperative of competitiveness. The scramble is on to deregulate. Governments have given up on the priority of providing for the disadvantaged and struggle instead to attract investment and create suitable enabling environments for business.

Now, there is clearly much to celebrate about allocative efficiency, the specialty of the marketplace, but it does not translate into distributive equity. Trade liberalization, policy reform and structural adjustment tend to concentrate wealth. Indeed, neither the gains, nor the losses from globalization have been evenly shared. Between the prosperous precincts of Crescentwood or Westmount and the struggling reserves of Shamattawa or Mashteuiash, between the comfortable suburbs of San Diego and the sprawling maquiladora export platforms just across the border in Mexico, we see sharper edges, deepening divides and widening chasms.

The point is that among the excluded, the exploited, the alienated and the marginalized — and a look at any hot air grating in downtown in winter will convince you that their numbers are growing — personal security is hardly flourishing. In an indirect but very real way, Canada's burgeoning population of street people and squeegy kids is a totem of globalization's social toll. And the Third World, once so distant, is now right here.

Internationally, the situation is somewhat parallel. Yes, we have an absence of formal international conflict, but in its place is a heavily armed peace, punctuated by frequent low intensity conflicts inside states and the occasional enforcement actions between them. These are the essential elements of what has been aptly dubbed the 'new world disorder'.

As polarization leaves an increasing number of citizens feeling economically distressed, politically disenfranchised, and prepared to embrace extremes, government priorities may, in the not too distant future, have to shift away from providing incentives to business and towards a more fundamental requirement: keeping the lid on. The problem, you see, with leaving more and more to markets is that whatever their virtues, and there are many, at the end of the day they are animated by greed and fear rather than rationality or compassion. They respond mainly to opportunity rather than need. Oscar Wilde probably said it best when he concluded that the problem with markets is that they can put a price on anything but a value on nothing.

On the home front and even in the face of post-deficit operating surplus, look not for a workable national day-care system, but for the continued expansion of the criminal justice system, proliferating correctional facilities and ever more heavily equipped security forces. What does one make of the arrests of protesters and incidents of pepper spraying in Vancouver? Perhaps what some have termed the residual state may end up looking more like a police state, or, after Singapore, a virtual police state … no social problems or violence, but strictly enforced limits on freedom of association and expression.

… global …
All of the observations offered above resonate deeply in Canada, which trade, travel and immigration figures suggest is among the most globalized countries on earth. This country's trading performance and general economic prospects have rarely looked better, and with the exception of employment, most macroeconomic indicators are pointing up. Our immigration program has delivered to this country a diverse array of talent and skills that has contributed enormously to this country's comparative competitiveness. This puts Canadians, at the very least, in an excellent position to offer other countries less experienced with globalization the benefit of lessons learned here.

But there is more. With rapid technological change, privatization, deregulation and policy reform in full swing, Canada is itself undergoing a form of structural adjustment. These changes have been accompanied by a predictable litany: the condition of public finances remains parlous, greater discipline is required to reduce debt, services must be further rationalized, taxes must be cut. Get government off our backs … Sound familiar?

National policies, expressed through approaches to medicare, social programming, pensions and income support, are facing relentless cost pressure and, in some cases, sustained attack from those favouring harmonization — usually a code for further reductions. Globalization has placed the discussion of comparative levels of social service front and centre in the domestic debate, and made the lowest common denominator relevant. This has in turn raised questions about the security accorded all areas of national policy specifically exempted under existing trade agreements.

And this goes well beyond the recent WTO ruling against Canada on the issue of split-run magazines. The present crisis over universality and access in health care, the outcome of which seems anything but a foregone conclusion, looks very much like a harbinger of things to come.

... but hanging on to what remains

By UN reckoning, Canadians continue to enjoy the highest quality of life in the world, to which a relatively small population, a rich resource base, and the historical inertia provided by relatively high levels of public service and effective planning and regulatory mechanisms have all contributed.

But broken windows and peeling paint in public schools, line-ups in hospital emergency wards, and a thousand program cuts suggest that this may be changing. I submit that the position of this country is far from secure; in even the once most favoured places — Argentina, Burma, Sri Lanka and elsewhere — things can and do go terribly wrong.

This is a land in which the dream of a politically distinct, economically coherent entity organized from East to West has largely given way to what some have described as the most potent iteration of the globalization process — the relentless southerly pull of continentalism, a process which in my view has been exacerbated by continuing decentralization. In these circumstances, what are the prospects for maintaining Canada's enviable quality of life, which has among other things served to attract duality foreign investment?

A weaker centre will be less able to establish the sorts of conditions which give rise to sustained prosperity. Governments are responsible for creating and maintaining the policy, institutional and infrastructural framework necessary for continuing economic development. So the question must be put: to what extent is globalization an obstacle to efforts to ensure for this country a secure place in the upper reaches of the new international division of labour? More on the foreign policy implications in a moment.

It has also been suggested that globalization could lead to an interpretation of Canadian social programs as investment subsidies, as some kind of offence against a level economic playing field. Is this sort of issue suitable for reference to one or another dispute settlement mechanism? Reversion to trade tribunals necessarily shifts the locus of decision-making responsibility away from parliamentarians and representative institutions. Are these technical bodies a likely source of enlightened public policy? Is transparency at risk? Globalization raises a host of fundamental public policy issues, too few of which are being publicly debated.

Looking out ...

I would like now to consider some of the public policy implications of the argument as presented so far, beginning with the observation that accelerating globalization, driven by markets, business and commerce, characterized by increasing economic integration and interdependence, carries major implications for national unity and domestic identity. So, too, for Canadian foreign policy. To recap, globalization has contributed, inter alia, to:

   1. reductions in the effectiveness and domain of the state and its powers, marked by constraints on sovereignty and a transfer of authority and legitimacy upwards, to supranational institutions, downwards, to lower levels of government, and outwards, to non-state actors, especially multinational corporations and NGOs;

   2. the rising importance of comparative quality of life and competitiveness, and the associated emergence of a new international division of labour which features increasing polarization and marginalization within and between countries and regions at all levels;

   3. a transformed international security situation, featuring a rise in the relative significance of human (as opposed to state) security indicators, with new threats ranging from market meltdowns to currency collapses, from virulent ethno-nationalism to uncontrolled migration, from terrorism to transnational crime, from environmental collapse to epidemic disease, and from climate change to diminishing biodiversity.

   It would be an understatement to suggest that all of this has engendered a requirement for innovative approaches to the theory and practice of diplomacy, development assistance, defence, conflict resolution, peacekeeping and peacebuilding. Each of these must be adapted, in some cases radically, to suit the changing circumstances outlined above.
   This is obviously not the time to offer a detailed analysis of those prospects. Suffice it for now to say that in my view Canada responded by setting aside broad, interrelated foreign policy themes and the pursuit of a wide-front human rights, democratic development, good governance agenda, in favour of seeking niches. In such areas as it has been determined that Canada might make a difference (for example land mines, child labour, small arms), this country now leverages such influence as it can muster through the application of 'soft power'.

This approach relies heavily on knowledge brokerage, media relations, NGO partnerships and coalition building with other elements of civil society, while placing less emphasis on more conventional instruments such as the military and the foreign service. McMaster Professor Kim Nossal has described this as "foreign policy on the cheap"; others believe it both appropriate and politically canny. The jury is still out.

There has also been an attempt to diversify Canada's growing dependence on the U.S. by reaching out to the Asia Pacific — with mixed results — and moving forward with other initiatives such as the FTAA. The negotiation of multilateral trade and investment agreements has assumed more importance generally. Here, too, however, it must be observed that the attempt to create a rules based, level playing field for international business has been hotly contested as both an unreasonable and unwise intrusion upon national sovereignty and a policy direction ultimately inimical to the public interest.

. . . and looking in

If all of this sounds rather like an extended lament ... it is. In my view, something worthwhile is being lost, and this should be recognized. But that is not to suggest that this is the time to bury our heads in the sand, embrace Luddism or attempt somehow to wrestle back the hands of time. On the contrary, I believe that any efforts to lock in the gains of globalization, or even to strategically resist some of its less appealing attributes, must begin with a full critical and analytical appreciation of the nature and dynamic of the process. Balance is essential, and to that end I have prepared an annex to this presentation entitled 'What's Good about Globalization'. This is not the place to dwell on those arguments, but they do merit consideration.

Nowhere is the double-edged quality of globalization more clearly revealed than in our own domestic situation. How so? Globalization continues to figure centrally in the spectre of separation, which haunts us still. To address effectively this most hardy of perennial issues, the federal government will have to go well beyond either Plan A or B and articulate a compelling vision of this country as something greater than the sum of its provincial parts. Any province electing to depart would then lose something more than its share of the whole, and all of us would emerge diminished.

Globalization is relevant to the unity file because it weakens states and is prejudicial towards precisely the types of programs and commitments required to give form and substance to the idea of Canada. The rigours imposed by fidelity to fiscal responsibility and balanced budgets have hobbled the capacity of the central government to act in the national interest and to elaborate an appealing vision of the whole.

The best argument is that resisting the force of globalization is proving difficult enough, even for the strongest. Would an independent Québec be better able to defend and protect its interests than has been possible within the larger framework of a united Canada committed to the promotion of bilingualism and biculturalism? Indeed, in the absence of the bulwark provided by the rest of Canada, I believe that Québec could face a cascade of new difficulties in areas with which it has had little direct experience, especially in foreign and trade policy, and defence.

Meanwhile, bereft of a francophone component, the remaining Canadian provinces would be hard pressed to find binding commonalities among themselves, and could well be individually attracted to some form of affiliation with the U.S.

In short, Canada as presently constructed finds itself — at minimum — in a better position to absorb losses and defend its core interests. Larger units are able to muster greater resources and to avail themselves of certain political economies of scale. Canada is already an extremely devolved federation; there is no reason that Québec's cultural and social aspirations cannot be fulfilled within a wider synthesis that compliments the determination of the rest of the country to remain united. Fragmented, all bets are off, and the divisive debates over language rights and partition are just the thin edge of the wedge.

There is also another, more controversial dimension involving the efforts of the government of Québec to achieve sovereign control over the province's political affairs, geographic territory, and destiny. This quest has been animated in large part by the majority of old stock — *pur laine* — Québecois who trace their roots back hundreds of years. Much, probably too much, has been made of the commentary directed at newer arrivals by some members of the Parti Québecois leadership around the time of the last referendum. Yet many observers, including many Québecois, have expressed concern over the appearance near the very centre of the sovereigntist cause not of territorial nationalism, but of a chillingly ethnocentric, exclusionary quality. What else can be made of slogans like '*le Québec aux Québecois*'?

In these and other respects the separatist project looks very much like a desperate rearguard action intended somehow to save Québec from the effects of globalization. Is that possible? Desirable? These are tough questions. Like most other dimensions of this complex and multi-dimensional process, globalization in the Canadian context cuts all ways.

Annex: What's good about globalization?
Scrolling through these images of a globalized cultural landscape, the picture seems rather desolate. It is ... and it isn't. There's a glimmering of light at the end of the tunnel, and it may be something other than an oncoming train.

At the end of the day globalization is driven less by political conspiracy than by market consensus. Motor vehicles, walkmans, fast food, slick films, glitzy retail — multinationals do what they can to manipulate markets and shape demand, but in large part they give people what they want — or think they want.

If globalization is the contemporary expression of a more familiar form of economic and political organization — empire — then it may, in the classic pattern, be sowing the seeds of its own undoing and laying the groundwork for the next phase of world history. For example, falling prices, growing market penetration and the absence of external controls have combined to greatly expand national and international communications. Anyone with access to a computer and modem can communicate with anyone with similar access, anywhere. Think of the Internet cafes which have sprung up across China, or the spirited accounts of RCMP excesses at the APEC meetings in Vancouver last November posted electronically for immediate global perusal.

All of this is profoundly subversive of hierarchy and control, supportive of the ethic of democracy, and conducive to the exchange of ideas. As Gwynne Dyer and others have illustrated, the triumph of representative democracies over authoritarian dictatorships looms as one of the major historical themes of the late twentieth century. Similar countervailing parallels can be adduced for many of globalization's more vexing dimensions.

This manner of analysis suggests that we may be caught in some kind of a temporary lag which presages passage towards a more balanced future. If so, there may already be some early signs of institutional catch-up. Serious consideration has been accorded to a proposal pitched by Yale University economist, James Tobin, to tax international financial transactions, with a higher rate assigned to short-term speculative flows. While this is an idea whose time is yet to come, implementation could produce revenues in the range of $100 billion/year, which could in turn be applied towards ... capacity building and debt reduction for the poorest? Hope springs eternal.

There have, in any case, been more concrete developments. Labour and environmental sub-agreements, however imperfect, were retrofitted into the NAFTA, are front and centre in discussions within the WTO, and, along with human rights, are even finding their way into the APEC process and

MAI negotiations. Trade unions, aboriginal confederations, human rights organizations and ecological advocacy groups are all working to internationalize their operations, and in so doing provide some counterweight to the status quo. It's a start.

CHRISTINE SHELLY

Christine Shelly worked for nearly thirty years in United States government service with the Department of State and Department of Defense. In the State Department, she was a member of the Senior Foreign Service, where she held the rank of Minister-Counselor. She spent the past five years on detail to the Department of Defense and the U.S. Army, serving as Deputy Commandant for International Affairs at the U.S. Army War College from 2002-2004.

Her prior political-military experience includes six years at the North Atlantic Treaty Organization (NATO) in Brussels between 1987 and 1993. During the intervening years, between 1996 and 1999, she served at the U.S. Embassy in Ottawa as Minister-Counselor for Political Affairs.

Her long and distinguished career also includes service as Deputy Spokesman and Deputy Assistant Secretary in the Bureau of Public Affairs. As Deputy and later Acting Spokesman, she regularly conducted the State Department press briefing. Her other Foreign Service assignments include: the U.S. Embassies in Lisbon, Portugal and Cairo, Egypt.

Her many honours include two State Department's Superior Honor Awards, and two Department of the Army Decorations for Distinguished Civilian Service. In 2001, she received the Foreign Service Institute's Adjunct Faculty Award in National Security Affairs and was selected by the Thomas Sorensen Institute for Political Leadership at the University of Virginia as a Senior Fellow.

Christine Shelly entered the Foreign Service in 1975 after completing M.A. and M.A.L.D. degrees at the Fletcher School of Law and Diplomacy at Tufts University. She speaks fluent French and Portuguese.

Ms. Shelly was acting U.S. ambassador when she gave this paper.

1999

The Challenges of Shared Security

by Christine Shelly

Introduction

MERCI. Je suis tres heureux de parler avec vous aujourdhui. C'est toujours un plaisir de me retrouver ici, même en plein hiver. I know many of you may be tired of hearing about my youth, but I can't help but note that I feel very much at home here having spent the first twelve years of my life growing up in Canada, in Montréal, in fact.

On so cold an afternoon, I would normally talk to a group like this about economic and trade issues. That can often be a good way of raising the temperature. Instead, I want to discuss another important aspect of our remarkably successful bilateral relationship — our partnership in ensuring the peace and security of the continent and the globe that we share. This security partnership is less tangible and receives much less acclaim than the billion dollars a day in trade and the hundreds of thousands of people who cross our common border each day, but it is just as important.

It is fitting that we should take a few moments, almost exactly one year since the historic Montréal ice storm of 1998 to reflect upon the extraordinary value of our joint military capability. In January of last year, the Canadian military, with a little help from their friends south of the border, demonstrated in glorious fashion that they could confront and conquer cold weather as well as cold war. Only twelve short months ago, the Canadian forces carried out their largest peacetime deployment ever: literally rescuing one region of the country from an unanticipated foe — Mother Nature.

Recognizing that together we face other foes around the world, some known, some suspected, I thought that I would spend a few moments with you discussing the importance of shared security; the ways in which we cooperate together to achieve security; and the need to ensure that we can maintain our remarkable partnership in the future.

The Importance of Shared Security

Les Etats-Unis et le Canada partagent des succèss extraordinaires, notamment en ce qui concerne la libre circulation entre nos deux pays ainsi que nos accords de libre-échange. Plusieurs de nos citoyens, en raison notamment des liens familiaux et personnels qui les unissent, ont à coeur l'état de nos relations bilaterales. A bien des égards, nous partageons ensemble un façon de vivre qui fait l'envie du monde entier.

A basic sense of security — not just the absence of war, but the genuine peace and good neighborliness that have blessed relations between our two countries for more than a century — is fundamental to the economic prosperity and way of life we have achieved in North America. The importance of security as a basis for not only economic and commercial activity, but virtually all of what we know as civil society, while often not discussed, is clear. A secure environment provides the conditions under which individual citizens can achieve what they most want — peace, order and good government in the case of Canadians; life, liberty and the pursuit of happiness in the case of my countrymen. Security is the bedrock on which we preserve our freedoms and build our economic prosperity.

But like bedrock, the security partnership we share is largely taken for granted here in North America. We have enjoyed a common security on this continent for so many years that we tend to assume that it always was and always will be this way.

In fact, history teaches us that we could not always take peace for granted in North America, and logic causes us to conclude that benign neglect or flawed assumptions could undermine our security in the future. In Canada, Martello towers and the Rideau Canal bespeak the threat felt by your side of the border — just as Fort Ticonderoga commemorates invasion of our territory from north of the 49th parallel. We are still painting the White House to hide the smoke stains caused when it was burned by troops down from Canada in 1814.

Fortunately, since the time the Rideau Canal was completed, we have experienced no military conflict across what has become known as the world's longest undefended border. Our two countries have demonstrated to the world that neighboring nations, while maintaining their sovereignty and distinct identity, can interrelate and interconnect in unprecedented commercial and societal ways to the tremendous benefit of both our peoples. However, like a good marriage, this historic relationship requires constant attention and effort. In fact, this may be a particularly critical time for the security aspect of our broader partnership as we continue to define the threats and the solutions in the evolving post Cold-War world.

The experience of the past half-century has taught us that our prosperity is linked, in fact, not just to the security of North America, but to that of our closest trading partners as well. Many students of European history and politics argue that the security (and resulting stability) that the North Atlantic Treaty provided to post– World War Two Europe enabled the rebuilding of shattered economies, laying a foundation for what is now the European Union to take root and flourish. That Europeans — who had only a few years previously been locked in bitter conflict — could band together with Canadians and Americans for collective defense was a remarkable achievement, the 50th anniversary of which will be celebrated next April. While NATO continues to evolve in recognition of the Post Cold War realities, there is much about NATO's traditional role and strategy which has served Canada, the United States, and the allies well over the decades and which does not require change, simply for change's sake. As we say in the South, "if it ain't broke, don't fix it."

The Post Cold War Era

The Cold War ended ten years ago, and we are all relieved to live in a more optimistic era. In the early years of this decade Canada and the U.S. sought to take advantage of the changed global security environment, as well as grapple with the problems of budget deficits, by cashing in on some of the so-called peace dividend. In my country's case, conventional and nuclear capability have been significantly reduced. U.S. defense spending fell from nearly US$306 billion at the beginning of this decade (about five per cent of GDP) to about US$270 billion (about 3.5 per cent of GDP). During the same period, Canada's defense spending fell from about C$13 billion to under C$10 billion (representing about 1.2 per cent of Canadian GDP).

The United States and Russia have made substantial cuts in their strategic weapons throughout the Strategic Arms Reductions Talks, and following consultations with Canada and other NATO allies, the United

States has moved resolutely since the end of the Cold War to dramatically reduce nuclear arms stationed in Europe. In fact, we have eliminated our nuclear weapons — and assisted in the destruction of Russian weapons — virtually as fast as physically possible. This is an extraordinary feat that is too often overlooked.

Despite the end of the Cold War and encouraging progress in nuclear disarmament, it would be naïve to believe that the world has been forever cleansed of conflict, that military forces are now anachronisms — or even that the peace and security of our two peoples has been permanently assured. I need not catalogue the conflicts that have occurred over the past ten years. Little imagination is needed to picture the world as it would be today if we and our allies had not maintained the means and the will to defeat Iraq's annexation of Kuwait — or to make peace in Bosnia. While the threats to peace and security in 1999 may be different from those of the Cold War era, it would be folly to conclude that the threats no longer exist.

New Risks

As the old threats pass from the scene, we face new challenges to our security. For example, we must be conscious of the new threat posed by the spread of technology which makes it easier and cheaper to build nuclear, chemical and biological weapons and long-range missiles. Such technology is readily available to countries whose record suggests that they may resort to these weapons whether such an action is rational or not.

While the face-off of competing nuclear superpowers may be behind us, more than twenty nations currently seek or possess some sort of medium range ballistic missiles. The recent North Korean missile test and detonation of nuclear devices in South Asia are clearly cause for concern.

The work of the United Nations Special Commission in Iraq — much of it publicly available — has illustrated graphically how far and how fast governments intent on building an arsenal of this nature can progress. Let me pause here to say how much the United States appreciates Canada's strong support for the work of UNSCOM, and for the recent decisive action required when Saddam Hussein repeatedly obstructed the work of the UN's arms inspectors.

In addition, unfortunately, we have reached a point in world history where 'non-state actors', groups which are not responsible to governments at all, now have potential access to devastating weapons. Over the generations, the world community has established international mechanisms, some more effective than others, to deal with nations which act or propose to act outside of acceptable norms. We must now determine whether the traditional frameworks and doctrines are adequate to address these novel threats.

Facing the Challenges

The U.S. and Canada continue to work together against the new risks to security around the world through such mechanisms as NATO and on the UN Security Council. In this hemisphere, we do so through our common participation in the Permanent Joint Board on Defense and North American Aerospace Defense Command, better known as NORAD.

A key element in our security partnership is the U.S./Canada Permanent Joint Board on Defense, the PJBD. If it is unfamiliar to you, the explanation lies in a lack of publicity, not in any lack of effectiveness. The PJBD was established in 1940 by President Roosevelt and Prime Minister Mackenzie King. Its mission was set out in the Ogdensburg Declaration signed by the President and Prime Minister: "to consider in the broad sense the defense of the northern half of the Western Hemisphere."

In practice, senior Canadian and American military and civilian personnel involved in bilateral defense have met and consulted on a regular basis for nearly sixty years on matters related to our shared security. With the end of the Cold War, the focus of the PJBD has changed, but not the principles of consultation and joint action to preserve shared security.

For example, the PJBD has recently taken up the issue of protection of critical infrastructure — power, communications, transportation and so on — from both natural and man-made disasters, such as the so-called 'millennium bug' that will affect some computers when their internal clocks roll over to January 1, 2000. Our critical infrastructure systems are so interlinked across our border that it is impossible to think only in terms of national plans to protect them. We have to think in terms of a North American plan. This collaboration was critical in response to the ice storm. At the request of the Canadian Forces, the U.S. military was able to deliver thousands of cots to affected areas. Also, several flights of our largest transport aircraft, the C–17, were used to move equipment such as field kitchens and large generators from Western Canada to the east.

Like the PJBD, NORAD is a unique American/Canadian institution. Established in 1958, NORAD formalized existing air defense agreements between the U.S. and Canada and created a binational command structure for air defense of North America. In practice this means that Canadian and American military personnel work side-by-side at facilities in both of our countries, sharing the authority and responsibility for joint defense at Cheyenne Mountain, Colorado, Winnipeg and other locations.

The greatest benefit our governments derive from NORAD is the ability to share resources and costs needed for aerospace security. It would be militarily and economically impractical for either nation alone to monitor and protect the airspace in which we have a joint interest.

Peace-Making and Peace-Keeping

The U.S. and Canada also work together to counter threats to security through peacekeeping, peacemaking and humanitarian operations outside of North America. We recognize Canada's particular focus on peacekeeping capability and are thankful for its application in such complex settings as Haiti.

The Challenges of Shared Security

So that is where we have been and what we have accomplished by being partners in the security of this continent and the globe. Let's now briefly examine what these lessons tell us about the future.

There is a clear and important lesson to be learned from our joint experiences, including the recent events in Iraq: diplomacy, while a vital tool, is not a complete solution to the problem of ensuring security, even in the post Cold-War era world. Nor are economic sanctions, UN resolutions, eloquent speeches, or the best of intentions and examples. At the turn of the century, President Theodore Roosevelt said that we should "walk softly but carry a big stick," a piece of advice as relevant now as when he said it. Diplomacy, to be effective, must be backed up with a credible ability to deter aggressors, to enforce agreements, and to ensure that the will of the international community is carried out. And our countries must be sure that we continue to have the capability to back up our aspirations and our words with action when necessary.

As partners in North American defense and peacekeeping elsewhere in the world, we both need high quality, well-equipped, professional defense forces, capable of undertaking all appropriate defense tasks separately, jointly, and in coalition with our allies. At one end of the spectrum, we need to be ready to cooperate in operations like Desert Storm, and at the other end we must be able to answer the call for peacekeepers. Yet even in peacekeeping, as our experience in Bosnia has shown, we must be prepared for operations involving a high degree of risk, requiring specialized training and equipment, and battle readiness. Peacekeeping oftentimes must be preceded by peacemaking.

Both of our countries took advantage of the end of the Cold War to balance budgets in part through reductions in defense. We were successful, and our budgets are now in surplus. In his address to the Canadian Parliament in 1995, President Clinton said: "There are those in both our nations who say we can no longer afford to, and perhaps we no longer even need to exercise our leadership in the world. And when so many of our people are having their own problems, it is easy to listen to that assertion. But it is wrong." The requirement for well-trained, well-treated, and well-equipped military forces will continue, because although the threats that we face now are quite different from those of a decade ago, we do not yet live in a perfect world.

Recent analyses by the executive and legislative branches of government in my country, as well as an extensive report by a Canadian Parliamentary Committee, have concluded that additional resources are required for our militaries because we both may have acted too quickly to reap the peace-dividend that accompanied the end of the Cold War. There is little doubt that equipment must be modernized, readiness must be enhanced, and personnel needs must be addressed. As President Clinton stated just ten days ago in announcing his decision to increase the U.S. military budget for the next fiscal year by twelve billion dollars, it is "not just the quality of our weapons, but the quality of our people in uniform" that makes the difference.

Canada and the United States will always share a huge number of common security interests — history and geography make that inevitable. We need to remember that preserving security is not cost-free, although I would argue that in the long run it is always cost-effective.

Policymakers must regularly confront tough choices. Investment in national security does not always pay immediate dividends, and may not have the same degree of vocal support as more domestic expenditures might. But history shows us that, much like the stock market, it pays off over the long run.

Ladies and gentlemen, as I observed at the beginning, security and prosperity are inextricably linked. We have — through our common efforts — enjoyed the blessing of many years of both. Our challenge is to continue to make the difficult decisions that will permit us to continue to work together in the world's most unique security partnership, to ensure that the generations that follow us will truly have the opportunity to enjoy peace, order, good government, along with life, liberty and happiness.

    Merci.

JAMES TAYLOR

James H. Taylor, widely known as 'Si', was born in Hamilton. Educated at McMaster University and, as a Rhodes Scholar, at Balliol College, Oxford, he joined the Department of External Affairs in 1953. His postings included Vietnam, India, France, Russia, Belgium and Japan.

Between 1982 and 1985, he served as Ambassador to NATO, and in 1989, became Canada's Ambassador to Japan. Between these two prestigious diplomatic postings, he served as Under Secretary of State for External Affairs.

Following his retirement, Taylor became Chancellor of McMaster University between 1992 and 1998. He is an Officer of the Order of Canada.

This paper was written as a foreign policy consultation for Foreign Minister Lloyd Axworthy.

1999

Canadian Foreign Policy and National Interests

by James H. Taylor

THIS PAPER IS INTENDED TO HELP define and promote the discussion of Canada's foreign policy interests. The interests in question are those of Canada as it now exists. Constitutionally, the country is a parliamentary democracy in a federal state. It has two official languages, French and English. Economically, it is a market economy. It is wealthy by world standards and relatively dependent on foreign trade, especially with the United States. It has a mixed population, including a high proportion of recent immigrants from around the world. The new arrivals are encouraged by official policy to maintain and pursue the cultural traditions of their countries of origin, to an extent compatible with their new circumstances. The majority of Canada's people live in towns and cities, scattered widely across a vast national territory. Much of the land is unsuitable for dense settlement. The climate is challenging. Bordering on three oceans, Canada has the longest coastline of any state in the world and the second largest national territory, but only one land neighbour — as it happens, the world's richest and most powerful state.

Canada is a strong state and stands at the top of the UN's Human Development Index. Among its strengths are the relative security guaranteed by its geographic position; the rich endowment of its natural resources; the quality and extent of its infrastructure, the opportunities afforded by its proximity to the United States; and the stability assured by its peaceable, well-educated population and sound social structures. Yet while it is praised and envied as one of the most successful countries on the planet, it has weaknesses and faults, and some of these are serious. For a generation, it has faced a fundamental threat to its existence from Québec separatism. Its federal union is uneasily balanced between pressures of centralization and decentralization. Its economy struggles with high debt, high taxes, low productivity and resource dependency. Its educational system delivers less than expected from the high investment in it. It is rich but prodigal in its use of energy, and the environmental quality of urban life is under stress. It wastes and mismanages other resources, depleting rather than stewarding them and polluting excessively in the process. Wealthy, it yet has many poor, a less than ideal distribution of income, and some badly strained social services. It struggles painfully with the problems of doing justice to its First Nations.

From this description, warts and all, much can be inferred about Canada's national interests. Most policy decisions about these interests will be decisions about domestic, not foreign, policy although foreign policy decisions will have deep domestic roots. Furthermore, it has to be remembered that decision-making in foreign policy, and the pursuit of established policy, are only a part of any country's total diplomatic effort, much of which is inevitably devoted to reacting to events abroad. That said, the task of foreign policy is to create, to the extent that it can, the external conditions that allow a country like Canada to flourish. In sum, foreign policy seeks peace and prosperity abroad in order to help Canadians build a peaceful, prosperous and just society at home.

Peace and Security

Thanks to its geography, Canada is one of the most secure countries in the world, and is likely to remain so as long as it retains good relations with the United States, with which it was last at war between 1812 and 1814. The nation as it emerged in the twentieth century had no unresolved border disputes, though its Arctic claims did not pass unchallenged. The development of the Law of the Sea over the past generation has altered this situation. By extending the territorial sea and creating an economic zone beyond it, the Law of the Sea has laid vast additional responsibilities on states like Canada and generated new conflicts over maritime boundaries and resources. Canada has unsettled sea and shelf disputes with the United States over both ends of the Alaska border, in the Beaufort Sea and Hecate Strait; in the Strait of Juan de Fuca; and around Seal Island in the Bay of Fundy. As well, the border between Canada and Greenland is not yet fully settled. Canada has managed to settle some such disputes, peacefully but with difficulty. Quarrels of this kind have demonstrated clear potential to disrupt relations with otherwise friendly countries such as the United States, France, Portugal and Spain. Unresolved disputes of this sort will demand political and diplomatic attention in future. Thus, for example, Canada will have to maintain sea and air forces adequate to patrol and protect fisheries and support the country's position in international law on the rights and responsibilities of maritime states.

In a similar way, intellectual and material resources will have to be found to deal with the international implications of transboundary pollution, as a complement to domestic programs to protect the environment.

Dealing with such issues may be difficult and expensive. But at their most troublesome, quarrels over maritime boundaries and resources or environmental protection should not of themselves pose dramatic threats to national security. Are there other threats that could?

Even during the Cold War, the idea of a direct attack on North America was imaginable only in the most extreme and unlikely circumstances; since the end of the Cold War, it has become so close to unimaginable that many people have simply stopped thinking about it. A certain residual queasiness about rogue Russians and the safety and security of Russian nuclear facilities is all that remains. Yet Canada continues to be committed in NATO and NORAD to the defence of North America. In theory, Canadians could decide to contribute nothing to continental defence, on the grounds that there is no point in wasting resources on meeting threats that don't exist. The United States would certainly not take such an attitude even if Canada did. It would go on defending North America and defending Canada in the act of defending itself. Not that Canadians are likely to support a policy of making no contribution to continental defence. That would surely be seen as a shameful abdication of a clear national responsibility and a threat to Canadian sovereignty. The hard questions are therefore what form the contributions should take. Whatever they may be over time, the consequences have to be lived with. The decision against equipping the navy with nuclear-powered submarines or building a nuclear-powered ice-breaker, for example, left Canada with a fleet largely unable to navigate in the Arctic and obliged to transfer units between Atlantic and Pacific on the surface through the Panama Canal.

In Europe, the original fear of a massive attack by Soviet conventional forces disappeared with the end of the Cold War. Canada quickly drew some of the necessary conclusions, withdrawing the forces it had long stationed in Germany. Yet Canada continues to be committed to the defence of an enlarged treaty area under NATO. Furthermore, it is now involved in new, wider arrangements to defend the treaty area from threats arising outside it. It has contributed to planning to meet such threats and from time to time contributes forces to operations accordingly, as in the former Yugoslavia. Meanwhile, Canada continues to debate with its NATO allies whether all the necessary conclusions from the end of the Cold War have been drawn, especially in the field of nuclear strategy (see, for instance, reports on this subject issued by the House of Commons Standing Committee on Foreign Affairs and International Trade in mid-December 1998).

The nuclear issue is complex and controversial. Some maintain that nuclear deterrence nowadays is like a religion in decline, its temples empty and its priests apostate; that 'as a belief system, [it] is close to collapse in the countries where it was invented.' Is this accurate? Or does the evidence suggest that the faith is still strong, especially among Canada's nuclear-armed allies, who will by no means be easy converts to a new doctrine? Most people were no doubt nothing but relieved to be able to stop thinking about the balance of terror and mutually assured destruction. They may not be thirsting to re-open the nuclear debate. If Canada decides to do so, however, it must make a respectable contribution. This is easier said than done.

Canadians would have to clear their minds on a number of difficult questions. When can we expect to see American and Russian stocks of nuclear weapons reduced to levels that remove the pretext they give other nuclear states to avoid disarming themselves? Meanwhile, how much pressure would Canada be prepared to exert on Britain, France, China, India and Pakistan, and what form should such pressure take? Should the ultimate objective be the complete destruction of all nuclear weapons, or something short of that? What needs to be done to ensure the security of existing stocks of weapons and prevent their further spread pending their eventual destruction, and what part should Canada play in such undertaking, whether multilaterally through the International Atomic Energy Agency or bilaterally? How are threats from other weapons of mass destruction and from conventional weapons (including small arms) best dealt with, assuming the progressive disappearance of nuclear weapons? And assuming nuclear power installations will remain even if nuclear weapons are abolished, what should be done to prevent other Chernobyls?

Some of these issues may appear arcane or hypothetical. We cannot respectably enter the debate, however, unless we are prepared to 'think our thoughts down to the roots'; to be prepared to do battle — at least intellectually. A price in effort and strained relations will no doubt be exacted.

However much or little Canadians may have thought about these matters since the end of the Cold War, they evidently want their government to go on working for the elimination of nuclear weapons and other weapons of mass destruction, and the reduction of conventional weapons. In recent years, progress in nuclear and even in conventional disarmament has been made that was inconceivable twenty years ago. Yet a viable international system much less dependent on high levels of armament may not be so utopian after all. This should be a stimulus to further efforts towards disarmament, particularly effective implementation and verification of existing agreements. Still, the present generation must expect to live out its lifetime in a world where serious unresolved questions of nuclear safety, nuclear proliferation and nuclear disarmament remain; where other weapons of mass destruction must still be reckoned with; and where large stocks of conventional weapons are readily available to those who choose to achieve their ends by force. The implications for Canadian policy of such an international security environment must be carefully thought through.

A further difficulty about the emerging security context is that, whereas formerly threats to security arose mainly from wars between sovereign states, they now arise more and more frequently from civil conflict within them. To deal effectively with this perplexing dimension of international security means revising traditional attitudes to national sovereignty. Some of the difficulties encountered with peacekeeping in Somalia, central Africa, and the former Yugoslavia illustrate the problem. So do the war crimes trials in The Hague and Rwanda and the proceedings against General Pinochet. The Canadian bias will no doubt be to support the trend towards diluting classic concepts of sovereignty. But national sovereignty has its reasons, and when pushed, Canadians have shown themselves every bit as jealous of their sovereignty as any other people. Presumably they will wish to proceed with caution, though Canada did not proceed particularly cautiously when pursuing the successful initiative for an international criminal court.

Furthermore, the rationale for intervening in little wars in far-off places, whether civil wars or not, has changed markedly since Canada became a sovereign state. Canadians entered the great period of postwar reconstruction of the international order persuaded that they were, so to speak, holding onto one end of a string of firecrackers which, if lit at the other, would explode up the string until the last firecracker blew up in their faces. The failure to prevent the Second World War suggested that aggression had to be nipped in the bud; otherwise little wars far away could become big wars near at hand. Moreover both world wars had spread geographically and grown in violence as they progressed. At the end of the second, weapons capable of destroying mankind were used. All this implied that peace was indivisible, and that any threat to security anywhere was a threat to everyone everywhere.

The Cold War showed this was not so. Conventional wars — for example, in Korea and Vietnam — were fought for years at high levels of conventional violence with the direct participation of nuclear weapons states and their allies. Yet these wars neither spread nor went nuclear. The conclusion was that not all little wars become big wars. Not all distant wars inexorably draw near. Not every Nasser — not even a Saddam Hussein, although the analogy is closer — turns out to be another Hitler. It thus has become harder to argue that Canada's national security interests are threatened by any act of aggression anywhere in the world, except in the most remote and attenuated sense. Since the end of the Cold War and the tendency of East-West rivalry to recruit partisans everywhere in the world, this has been even more the case. Peace, it seems, is not indivisible at all; quite the contrary.

Yet Canada continues to contribute to suppressing violence and turning back aggression far from its borders. Since such interventions can no longer be justified on the grounds of any substantial threat to national security, they must be rationalized on other grounds — humanitarian considerations, or the defence of human rights, or the fulfillment of obligations under the UN Charter. Perhaps the underlying rationale is even simpler. It may have to do with Canadians' self-image, and their faith that, most of the time, peace is good, war is bad, and that those who enjoy peace themselves have a moral obligation to do what they can to see that others are allowed to live in peace also. If so, the peace Canadians seek is their own peace of mind. But this is more a matter of altruism than interest.

Prosperity and Economic Relations

Canadians expect their government to ensure the country's steadily increasing prosperity, and to act to influence the international economic environment accordingly. This is from some points of view an easy interest to serve; Canada is an attractive economic partner. It has a wealthy economy, highly dependent on foreign trade and open to it. It is a source of a wide range of raw materials, as well as finished goods and services of high quality at competitive prices. It is on the whole an attractive field for foreign direct and portfolio investment, and it needs to be able to exchange people, ideas, technology, goods, services and capital with the minimum of government intervention required to ensure stability, legality and equity in the markets.

In recent years, Canada has made good progress in correcting some notorious weaknesses, notably in reducing excessive levels of public deficits and debt. But compared to some other industrialized countries, it is criticized at home and abroad for high taxes, low productivity, high unemployment, a weakening currency relative to the U.S. dollar, and the persistence of some barriers to trade and investment, especially interprovincially. To the extent this criticism is justified, remedies lie largely in the realm of domestic policy; abroad, one of the government's tasks is to ensure that foreign governments and foreign markets are given a balanced picture of Canada's political and economic prospects. It must, for example, persuade those with influence over international financial markets to review the accuracy of their assessment of this country's degree of dependence on commodity exports, a judgment which in turn impacts on Canada's credit rating and currency valuation.

By far the most important single element in Canada's foreign economic relations is the relationship with the United States, which is the largest of its kind in the world. Canada is overwhelmingly dependent on the U.S. as an export market and very heavily dependent on it as a source of imports, whether of goods, ideas, technology or capital. No Canadian province, with the exception of British Columbia, has foreign economic partners that come anywhere near matching the United States in their importance to the local economy. To have unhindered, trouble-free access to the world's closest, richest and most open market is a vital Canadian interest. Happily, such access is, broadly speaking, available most of the time. Many Canadians, however, have viewed this dependence with alarm, as a factor of national weakness and vulnerability. Over the years, several governments have sought to reduce this vulnerability by leading a search for alternatives. In different ways, both Prime Ministers John Diefenbaker and Pierre Elliot Trudeau made such an attempt. So did Brian Mulroney, not in the form of a search for alternative markets, but in the form of seeking more secure access to the American market under the Canada-U.S. Free Trade Agreement.

Whatever the impact of different government policies — a question much disputed — the fact is that Canada's export dependence on the U.S. market, for good or ill, has risen in the lifetime of older Canadians from two-thirds to three-quarters to over four-fifths of total exports. Japan, Canada's second-largest national trading partner has never taken more than about eight per cent of Canadian trade. While the vast bulk of Canada-U.S. trade takes place smoothly with a minimum of government intervention, the enormous scale of the relationship guarantees that, at any one time, Canada and the United States will be at odds over one or another well-publicized trade dispute. Relative to this scale, however, Canada's trade with the United States is no more troublesome than it is with any other major trading partner; if anything it is less. Here indeed lies the danger. With secure access most of the time for the whole range of its exports to the world's richest, most open and successful economy, and with a minimum of language and cultural complications to inhibit trade, Canada has few incentives that encourage suppliers to look beyond the United States for markets. This is despite the fact that Canadians who have learned to compete successfully in such a demanding market as the United States are well on their way to competing successfully elsewhere in the world.

All of the above suggests a set of priorities lie in Canada's foreign economic relations. As an open market economy dependent on free flows of goods, knowledge and capital, Canada must work to strengthen the international rules governing trade, capital movements, and intellectual property in ways congenial to national economic success. Bilaterally, the priority will inevitably be the United States, since what may appear even to be a minor technical dispute against the background of the total relationship can nonetheless have dire repercussions for many Canadians. No government can hope to modify substantially, let alone reverse, the economic integration of Canada with the United States. For all the benefits of the Canada–United States relationship, many Canadians will remain uneasy, even alarmed, about this degree of dependence. Governments will be under pressure to seek alternatives or counterweights. While the sum total of Canada's other foreign economic relations will never come near matching the weight of the relationship with the United States, economic ties with other countries and regions will be important not only as the alternative markets and sources of imports and capital they provide, but psychologically, by giving Canadians a reassuring sense that not all their economic eggs are in the American basket.

Meanwhile, it will be important to ensure the effective management of Canada-United States bilateral trade and economic issues in circumstances where the weights of the two partners will always be greatly unequal. This is no easy task for governments. The sheer volume and complexity of exchanges between the two countries, to say nothing of the prevailing public philosophy and the general informality of relations, have limited the development of formal institutions and structures. Nonetheless, there are examples, from the International Joint Commission to the North American Free Trade Agreement, of areas constrained by formal undertakings. To the extent these constraints serve to isolate contentious areas, they reduce their potential to damage relations in general. By distancing themselves from the vagaries of the American political system, they compensate for the fact that no foreign partner, however skilful his diplomacy, will have the advantages enjoyed by a domestic lobby in the United States. At the same time, it will be important to ensure the effective operation of multilateral economic institutions that serve to keep all Canada's trading partners, and especially the United States, committed to and constrained by a rules-based international trade and financial system.

Economic relations with developing countries will always stand to some degree outside this framework. These relations occupy only a small part of Canada's total foreign economic ties. Nonetheless they loom larger in the public imagination than in statistics of trade and capital movements; in their expression as aid programs, they have usually enjoyed strong public support. It would be easy to demonstrate that, on a narrow view of Canada's interests, these programs have not always deserved the support the public had been prepared to give them. Aid can be used as a form of export subsidy for Canadian suppliers, but it is not normally a cost-effective form of promoting industry. Involved here is the counterpart in economic terms of the Canadian attitude to peacekeeping described earlier: Canadians' self-image and self-respect encourage them to the view that rich countries have a moral obligation to help poor countries. Whether this attitude serves an immediate economic interest or not, it is seen as a contribution in a broader sense to creating a more prosperous and secure world.

Society and Culture

Security and prosperity will provide the stable context and the flow of resources to build a better society. A basic contribution to the construction of this better society is made by immigration. The birthrate among Canadians is so low that, without immigration, the population would eventually shrink and age even more rapidly than is now the case. Immigration policy makes no distinctions on grounds of race, religion, colour or national origin. But it does make other distinctions and these affect Canada's external relations: if we decide, for example, to favour family class immigrants over entrepreneurs; or if we shift our recruiting efforts abroad from one place to another; or if we fix immigration levels more or less arbitrarily rather than on a rational calculation, there will be an impact on our ties with other countries.

However we choose to administer our immigration program, and whatever the priorities we set, immigration functions to link Canada ever more widely with the world. Internally it raises questions about the assimilation of newcomers into Canadian society; externally, about relations with the countries of origin of Canada's increasingly varied population. It is a commonplace to say that Canada is a multicultural country, a mosaic rather than a melting pot. An examination of the social realities that might justify this distinction, which is used frequently to distinguish Canada from the United States, would be timely and useful. It is clear, however, that there are limits to applying multiculturalism in both domestic and foreign policy.

Multiculturalism allows everyone to take pride in his origins. There are to be no second-class citizens in Canada. And multiculturalism in practice should mean more than government-subsidized folk dancing. But not every piece of imported culture can be set in the Canadian mosaic. For example, other languages will be valued, but there are only two official languages in Canada. Citizens who do not acquire one or the other risk being marginalized. Or again, by Canadian standards, the status of women is quite unsatisfactory in a number of the patriarchal societies that provide immigrants to Canada. Canadians would consider it a perversion of the notion of respect for other cultures were they expected to lower the status of women in their own society to accommodate what may be a fact of social life in the ancestral societies of some new citizens. So too, Canadians want to be generous in accepting genuine political refugees. But they would be appalled if their openness were to be abused to the point where Canada was to become a byword for openness to terrorist organizations, insurrectionary plotting, extortionate fund-raising and arms smuggling.

Even the legitimate advocacy of ancestral causes cannot imply a blanket endorsement by the Canadian government of every foreign quarrel the country imports along with its immigrants. The mere fact that particular Canadians may have an ancestral link with some foreign quarrel does not of itself define a Canadian interest. To act on the opposite assumption would be a recipe for foreign policy chaos. The government would find it impossible to choose between the mutually exclusive claims of Canadian Serbs and Croats, Russians and Ukrainians, Sikhs and Hindus, Hindus and Muslims, Arabs and Jews, Irish Nationalists and Irish Unionists, Tamils and Sinhalese, Turks and Armenians, and so on. Yet the government is often pressed, on grounds of multiculturalism, to accord such endorsements.

Multiculturalism must somehow be managed so that the construction of a better society in Canada is not disrupted. Legitimate ancestral pride and sentimental links with other countries cannot become a pretext for importing quarrels into Canada or disrupting the country's foreign relations. There may be legitimate and practical opportunities to draw upon multicultural resources to help other countries solve their problems. In political affairs, however, non-intervention and neutrality may often be the only sensible policy, given the varied composition of Canada's people.

Bilingualism and multiculturalism are facts of Canadian life that have become national policies, and as such, they are not without controversy. They are valued because they serve to protect distinctions that people care about in an age when many feel threatened by cultural homogenization. The various expressions of this mass civilization have become clichés of social analysis: Hollywood, CNN, the Internet, world money markets — these are the outlines of the borderless world in which cultural identities are dissolved. Much of this world was created in the United States. Canadians can take some comfort from realizing that they are not the only ones disturbed by this sort of cultural leveling of American origin. The same type of anxiety exists in countries as culturally secure as France and Japan. And of course, thousands of people in the United States itself are not particularly satisfied with the quality of the civilization they are accused of foisting on the world. English-speaking Canadians particularly feel vulnerable in the borderless world, since it leads them to wonder what of importance will remain in a few generations to distinguish Canada from the United States.

Some of these fears are surely neurotic, and would benefit from detached analysis. Free trade was always resisted on the grounds that it would lead to Canada's absorption by the United States. To what extent have these fears proven to be justified in practice? If our social safety net has holes in it, to what degree is this due to economic integration with the United States? Our cultural industries, we have decided, must be protected and subsidized if they are to survive in the face of pressures from the United States particularly. But how much of this problem is new, and how rapidly is it getting worse? What, for example, would a history of immigration patterns in North America reveal about the drain of talent from Canada to the United States over time? Are we worse off, from the point of view of Canadians' sense of themselves, than we were when Mary Pickford went to Hollywood, or John Kenneth Galbraith went to Harvard, or Wayne Gretsky left the Edmonton Oilers for the Los Angeles Kings? How much does it matter to the national psyche that the CFL may not survive in the television age? And how likely is it that the NHL may become almost entirely American? Does it matter whether Mavis Gallant lives in Paris whereas Margaret Atwood lives in Toronto, so long as what they both write is available around the world and reflects a Canadian sensibility? Some forms of cultural expression never had borders anyway — music spoke a universal language long before the world wide web was invented. Yet even posing these questions reveals a deep and genuine anxiety.

Presumably Canadians would like to have it both ways: to have a recognizably distinct national culture, protected if necessary, but not at the price of settling for some second-rate provincial version unfit to hold up its head in international company. The best exponents of this cultural identity will have to be free to come and go. Canada should continue to be a country that knows how to welcome a Dutoit or a Zuckerman or a Bissoondath. Equally, it must be a country that gives young Canadians a good start and continues to applaud their success whether they remain in the country or find eventually that, to develop their potential to the full, they must, like Norman Jewison, Dianne Telle or Michael Ignatieff, leave Canada to live abroad.

Here again, decisions affecting cultural policy will be domestic policy decisions with implications for foreign policy. This is true whether Canada decides to alter its tax laws to encourage donations to the arts or to help professional sports recruit stars and orchestras to recruit conductors; whether we decide to protect Canadian magazines or enforce Canadian content rules on TV and radio; whether we make it easier and cheaper for students to attend universities with better research facilities and higher-paid professors. All such decisions alter our relations with other countries. Each shapes an element of national interest that must be weighed in our external relations.

Conclusion

For a country that was never, to use an old-fashioned phrase, a Great Power, Canada has an extraordinarily wide set of international connections. This is as much a matter of historical inheritance as of calculated interest — the sheer accident that we share with some hundred countries in the world the experience of having been either a British or a French colony — and in Canada's case, both. Over time, Canadians have developed the network of their international ties, in part based on this historic inheritance, often synthesizing interests where none had at first existed. Among their other benefits, these connections help Canada escape what otherwise would be a too confining, too exclusive relationship with one mighty neighbour. They form part of an eternal search for options, alternatives and counterweights to the relationship with the United States. The attractiveness of these options changes constantly. Asia has dazzled, then dismayed us in the last decade. The same pattern may emerge vis-à-vis Latin America. Will Europe now open new horizons for us as the European Union evolves, or will Europeans have less time for Canada, given their own preoccupations?

Finally, a word or two on the crucial relationship among values, policies and interests. Some may be uncomfortable with the discussion of a policy development process that starts by defining interest. They might prefer to start with values. The two words have different overtones in foreign policy. Interests suggest things that can be defined, that have sharp edges, that are capable of being bargained over, that are material for compromise. Values suggest things more elevated yet softer in outline, things that are matters of principle and ideology, that are not good material for bargaining and compromise. In this sense, interests are a subject of diplomacy, whereas values are a subject of rhetoric.

At present, our values seem secure enough at home and under no severe threat from abroad. Core Canadian values are often said to include compassion, tolerance, civility, fairness, respect for diversity and the rule of law, and support for democracy. These values have been translated into more specific activities in support of interests, mainly humanitarian, and expressed as disaster relief and emergency assistance, development aid and human rights advocacy, refugee resettlement and environmental activism, and so forth. Each is or has been an important component of Canadian foreign policy.

So, too, it is with matters of political and economic security. Here, the engagement of our values and interests requires, among other things, coping with the actions of Saddam Hussein, the ideas of Mahathir Mohammed, the implications of chronic conflict in central Africa, and our own doubts about the benefits of the untrammeled operation of free markets. Of course, our international life would be more comfortable if more people shared our values, however much the effort to persuade them might raise difficult questions about the limits of proselytizing and ideological warfare. In any event, we may be sure that the defence of our values begins at home, and that we shall never be able to persuade others to adopt our values unless these are seen to be a living reality in our own society. This is yet another point where domestic performance and foreign policy intersect.

While there is ample scope in foreign policy for the free play of altruism and idealism, it must be added that the pursuit of values is often consonant with national interests, especially when those values are challenged or under attack, as was the case during the Cold War. In such circumstances, values and interests again converge. On the other hand, there sometimes arise occasions when the pursuit of interests is less clearly aligned with key values, as could be argued occurred during the 1994-95 'Fish War' with Spain, or in the case of Canada's aggressive bidding on commercial opportunities associated with the Three Gorges hydroelectric project in China.

In the end, and at its best, the formulation and implementation of effective foreign policy requires the judicious and informed balancing and rebalancing of interests through the prism of values. The identification of options, moreover, and the establishment of priorities in the face of competing objectives is at the best of times a difficult task. In today's complex and rapidly changing environment, which is exacerbated by limited and sometimes reduced foreign affairs resources, ambiguity will remain as a constant. Yet choices will have to be made, and they will in the long run be sustained by the public only if the options and the costs are made explicit.

At what point, for instance, do we stop a bilateral aid program in a poor country when it has come to mean pouring money down the drain? How anxious are we to trade if trade means accepting, or implicitly condoning, child labour or violations of human rights? How many Canadian jobs, on the other hand, would we be prepared to lose, if it came to that, in support of the rights of others? How far are we willing to see the lives of Canadian peacekeepers put at risk in quarrels that can only, by the greatest stretch of the imagination, be considered a threat to our national security?

These dilemmas come with the world-wide territory Canadians are obliged to deal with, voluntarily or involuntarily. Most will be hard to resolve; some will never be. But the search for solutions begins with an attempt to define Canada's interests in each situation.

Whatever the future may hold, the structure Canadians have consciously developed from the geography and history they inherited is now, after two generations of fully sovereign national life, world-wide and complex enough to throw up not just interests, but conflicts of interest. The more present Canada decides to be in this world, the more often Canadians will be called on to judge, to trade off, and to compromise. For Canada to remain secure and to prosper in the coming millennium, Canadian diplomacy will require, at minimum, great leadership and skill. The full benefit of our considerable experience abroad will need to be harnessed and brought directly to bear in establishing Canadian foreign policy priorities for the twenty-first century.

Margaret Catley-Carlson

Margaret Catley-Carlson currently chairs the Global Water Partnership, which links water management professionals worldwide, as well as the Water Policy Advisory Committee and the Centre for Agriculture and Bioscience International.

During her long career in economic development, she has served as president of CIDA, the Canadian International Development Agency, Deputy Director of UNICEF and president of the World Population Council. Her focus on education, health and resources has literally made a world of difference for women and children in many of the globe's poorest nations.

Born in Nelson, B.C., Margaret — or Maggie, as her friends call her — is married to Stan Carlson.

This paper was given to a large audience at the 1999 Pan American Games Women's Conference.

1999

Women in the Twentieth and Twenty-First Centuries

by Margaret Catley-Carlson

I. Challenges and achievements in the last thirty years: big pictures, big lists

I LIKE LISTS; they can say a lot if we learn to read the reality behind them. I want to give you a wide scope view of what has been happening in the world. I'm going to focus in on some of the challenges ahead in this hemisphere for the families of the hemisphere — and particularly for women. Then we'll talk about something that acts as a mirror in reflecting the situation of women and families; that is the phenomenon of global population growth.

A. Thirty short years ago in the whole developing world:
1. Approximately fifty-three per cent of the people were illiterate.
2. The average woman had six children.
3. About one in eight children died every year.
4. On average, four out of ten people suffered from malnutrition.
5. Close to three out of ten people did not have access to clean water or sanitation.
6. Every four out of five developing countries were not democracies.
7. Annual per capita income was about $700.
8. More than half of the people lived on less than a dollar a day.

B. Today in the developing world:
1. Literacy has risen by almost fifty percent.
2. Women have on average just under three children.
3. The infant mortality rate has been cut fifty percent.

4. Nearly five million fewer children die every year.
   5. Malnutrition has been cut by more than fifty percent.
   6. The percentage of people with clean water has tripled; access to sanitation has doubled.
   7. The scourge of apartheid has officially disappeared, though problems remain.
   8. Life expectancy has risen more than a decade.
   9. An additional seventy-one nations have moved to democracy or to more representative forms of government.
   10. Per capita income has risen by sixty percent.
   11. The percentage of those in absolute poverty has been cut almost in half.

This is really stunning success, given all considered. In the words of this conference, these are indeed achievements to celebrate.
   1. Conditions in the developing world have improved more in the second half of the twentieth century than in the previous 500 years.
   2. Some three to four billion of the world's people have experienced substantial improvements in their standard of living; and between four and five billion have access to basic education and health care.

C. There are real challenges ahead:
Lest we think the toughest tasks are over, here's the parallel list from the last two:
   1. One in eight plant species are threatened with extinction.
   2. More than 800 million people still face malnutrition.
   3. One quarter of the developing world's people still live in poverty — 1.3 billion have incomes of less than $1 per day.
   4. Nearly 140 countries share five percent of the private foreign investments flows that are now estimated at $250 billion annually, whereas a mere twelve countries get eighty per cent; clearly much remains to be done in creating positive investment climates.
   5. Latin American income differentials are worrying and growing.
   6. More than 100 million children are still not in school; the Western Hemisphere has done much better here — but quality of education is emerging as a problem in the globalizing world.

7. Over 180 million children under the age of fourteen work as child labourers.
8. There is continuing conflict in thirty countries.
9. About seventy percent of the people living in poverty are women.
10. At least 5,000 new HIV infections occur DAILY around the world.
11. An area the size of a soccer field is being destroyed every SECOND.
12. Every month the world's population still increases by the equivalent of all Canada's big cities combined.
13. Malaria kills a child every thirty seconds.
14. The richest twenty per cent of the population
    — Buys nine times as much meat
    — Has access to nearly fifty times as many telephones
    — Buys eighty times the paper products and motorized vehicles than the poorest twenty per cent (yet the poor are the ones chiefly hurt by air and water pollution).
15. More than 100 million people are poor in the world's richest nations. In the last decade, Canadians have been surprised and shocked to learn of the extent of poverty in our own country — and that one out of five children in our schools are struggling against the difficulties that poverty brings: difficulty concentrating, self-esteem, health problems and no access to resources.

II. FAMILIES AND THE CENTURY AHEAD: MYTHS AND REALTIES

A. Families in the future

What do we know for certain about families and women in the next century? If we trace today's trends forward we can see that the balance of economic responsibilities in families is shifting. Changes in the global economy are resulting in declining prospects for men in the labor market and increasing possibilities for women to work in both the less developed and industrialized worlds.

1. Women in all types of households — not only women officially designated 'household heads' — carry significant economic responsibilities; mothering is about earning as much as it is about nurturing. A rising proportion of households with children have a single parent, usually the mother.
2. While marriage remains a popular institution everywhere, it is also a fragile one for many people, falling short of a lifelong

partnership under one roof. Many children do not spend their childhood with both mothers and fathers.
3. Average household and family size — and therefore family support networks —are decreasing as a result of declining fertility rates and dispersal of family members. The dependency burden on working adults is intensifying (despite the drop in fertility rates) because of the extended period of childhood and the increased investments needed to prepare children to enter the modern economy.
4. Marriage and childbearing are being deferred to later ages.
5. It would be a pleasure to report that public policy in most countries reflects these quickly changing realities. In fact, policy is too often based on very powerful myths — you know these — we think we live by them.

THE MYTHS:
- The family is a stable and cohesive unit.
- Children live with their mother and father.
- Fathers serve as economic providers.
- Mothers serve as emotional caregivers.
- All children in a family are treated equally and well.

AND THE FACTS?
- There is a striking increase in single-parent families (mostly mothers) in the industrialized world and in the households headed by women in many developing countries.
- These increases are caused by high levels of marriage breakdown in developing countries, rising divorce rates in the industrialized world, childbearing by unmarried women, particularly adolescents, and migration by a spouse seeking employment.
- One parent, usually the mother, headed a quarter of households with dependent children in the United States in the 1980s. This is doubling every fifteen years.
- Surveys of Latin American and Caribbean countries showed a range in the proportion of households headed by women from thirteen per cent in Mexico to twenty per cent in Trinidad and Tobago. In Brazil, the percent of households headed by women rose forty-four per cent over ten years, from fourteen to twenty per cent.

- Even in households where fathers are present, mothers have increased economic responsibility for children. Changes in the global economy have resulted in a steadily rising number of women in the labour force, declining male employment, and an increasing proportion of two-earner families in both the industrialized and developing worlds. Women in all types of households make substantial and increasingly measurable economic contributions. Mothers may be the primary or sole support of families even where a father is present.

B. Global levels of marital dissolution are actually much higher than commonly believed, as a result of abandonment, separation, divorce or death of a spouse.
1. In the United States fifty-five of every 100 marriages end in divorce.
2. Divorce rates have more than doubled between 1970 and 1990 in Canada — and we are not alone — the same has happened in France, Greece, the Netherlands, the United Kingdom, and the former West Germany.
3. In developing countries an average of about twenty-five per cent of first marriages end by the time women are in their forties, as a result of divorce, separation or death.

C. A significant number of children in both rich and poor countries is born to mothers while they are unmarried, and this proportion is rising throughout the world. When the unmarried mother is an adolescent, the consequences for both mother and child can be especially severe, with impacts on the education of women, bonds between partners, relations with families, economic security and the child's healthy development.
1. In Northern Europe more than one-third of all births are to unmarried mothers; in Western Europe more than sixteen per cent; in United States twenty-eight per cent.
2. In Bolivia, Colombia, and Paraguay more than ten percent of unmarried women have had children.
3. Bonds between unmarried, pregnant, adolescent women and the fathers of their children are typically weak, even when the relationship leads to marriage.

D. Children in single-parent households are much more likely to be poor than those who live with two parents, largely because of the loss of economic support from absent fathers.
  1. In Chile, a study found that forty-two per cent of fathers of children born to adolescent mothers were providing no child support six years after the child's birth.
  2. In Jamaica, a father is held responsible for providing child support only to the children with whom he lives, who may not necessarily be his biological offspring.

E. In short, women worldwide are carrying an increasing share of economic responsibility for their children, and becoming the sole or most substantial economic support to a large proportion of the world's families.
  1. Mothering is about earning as much as it is about nurturing; being a mother may be the most important factor disposing women to poverty unless women's family roles are more fully called and responsibility for children is more equitably balanced between men and women.
  2. Fathers' roles overall have been neglected and much policy has operated as if children have a single parent — the mother, though there is considerable evidence that children benefit from the father being more involved in raising the child.
  3. Even though fertility is declining worldwide, the dependency burden on working parents has increased and significant numbers of the world's children suffer due to adverse family circumstances beyond their control.

F. There are policy initiatives that can strengthen family ties:
  1. Laws can protect parents who have custody of children against loss of land, housing or income.
  2. Strategies relating to employment and child care can help to accommodate the joint demands of work and home life for both men and women;
  3. Community-level services can support the poorest and most isolated parents. Young unmarried mothers, often abandoned by the fathers of their children as well as their families, should not feel they are also abandoned by society.
  4. We should all teach girls that they are likely to be economically responsible for themselves and their children at some point in their lives.

    5. We must teach boys that fatherhood includes making economic contributions to one's children and sharing responsibility for child care.

G. We also need to take a real look at young girls — now. [As small children] girls are the subject of much concern and then go off-screen until they become mothers. So a little attention to girls would go a long way.
    1. Girls should be educated to increase their economic productivity, improve their health, delay their age at marriage, lower fertility, increase political participation, and generally make more effective investments in the next generation.
    2. Girls should learn that their wages will rise by between ten and twenty per cent for each year of schooling they have beyond a basic education.
    3. Education enhances women's productivity in both the farm and non-farm sectors.
    4. Four years of school boosts a farmers' annual productivity by an average of nine per cent.
    5. In the urban sector, there is a positive association between education and earnings.
    6. Educated women have lower desired and actual family size. They are also much more likely to use contraception and have longer intervals between births. Among married couples, the wife's education has a much stronger effect on fertility than the husband's.
    7. In Asia, Africa and Latin America, women with seven or more years of schooling have two to three children less than women with up to three years of schooling.
    8. In Latin America and Asia, well-educated women are increasingly having the number of children they want.
    9. In Peru and Brazil, women with no education have about six children, while women with a secondary education have an average of three children.

H. Sports programs should not be overlooked, for they create opportunities to develop self-esteem, master new skills, and formulate a sense of body integrity.
    1. Understanding the complex relationship between a young women's body, her self-image and her reproductive health is

central to the promotion of health and healthy behavior.
2. Sports provide girls with the opportunity to master new skills, to have fun, to accept challenges, to compete and to experience the joy of movement.

III. THE POPULATION PICTURE: IT'S ALL ABOUT WOMEN

A. Population growth, is it a threat? Yes and no, if we let it be.
1. A revolution in reproductive behavior has swept the globe since the 1960s. In the developing countries of Asia, Africa, and Latin America contraceptive use, once rare, is now widespread and the average number of births per woman has fallen by half – from the traditional six or more, to just under three today.
2. In the industrialized world, already low fertility has dropped below two children per woman. This unprecedented development has led the UN to revise downward its latest forecast of world population. As a result, some fear a 'population implosion' or claim that 'the world population explosion is over'.
3. Instead of being near the end of the 'explosion' with today's population of about six billion, we are in fact just past its midpoint, according to the newly revised UN projection. After a record-breaking increase of two billion people over the past twenty-five years, the same increase is projected over the next twenty-five years, and a further expansion to some number between eight and ten billion is expected by 2100.
4. Nearly all of this growth will occur in the developing countries, where four-fifths of the world's population lives. Despite plummeting fertility rates, large increases are expected in Africa, Asia and Latin America for three reasons:

• First, the average decline from six to three births per woman still leaves fertility about fifty per cent above the two-child level needed to bring about population stabilization. With more that two surviving children per woman, every generation is larger that the preceding one. As long as that is the case, population expansion continues.

• Second, declines in mortality — historically the main cause of population growth — will almost certainly continue. Higher standards of living, better nutrition, expanded health services, and greater investments in public health measures have increased life expectancy by fifty per cent since 1950; a further rapid rise is likely. The unhappy exceptions will be mostly in those sub-Saharan African countries with severe AIDS epidemics. Also, as more people live longer, there will be more people alive.

- The final and most important factor is what demographers call 'population momentum'. This refers to the tendency for a population to keep growing even if fertility could immediately be brought to the replacement level of 2.1 births per woman (with constant mortality and zero migration). The reason for this growth is a young population age structure, which includes the historically largest generation of women about to enter the childbearing years. These women will produce more than enough births to maintain population growth for decades, even if they each have only two children. Further large increases in the population of the developing world are therefore virtually certain.

   5. Population growth is now one of the global issues most amenable to solution. Some investment is needed but the direction of change is positive; the question is the rate of acceleration of positive change.
   6. The package of investment measures that will make an impact has to do with girls – with supporting youth programs, especially those related to credit, gender, training, and vocational activities for young people. Special targeting for girls is needed.
   7. Europe, North America, and Japan face quite a different demographic population decline because measured fertility has remained below the replacement level since the mid-1970s. Though populations in most developed countries are still growing today (due to population momentum, rising life expectancy and immigration), reductions in population numbers are likely if fertility remains below replacement.
   8. The UN expects this decline to begin in Europe in 2000 and in Japan in 2005, while the populations of the U.S., Australia, Canada and New Zealand are expected to grow until at least 2050 (again, mainly due to immigration). For the developed world as a whole, population size is projected to rise slowly until 2025 and then decline, leaving the total in 2050 about the same as today.
   9. The proportion of the population over age sixty-five is expected to rise to twenty-five per cent in 2050, up from fourteen per

cent today. This trend will make it increasingly difficult for nations to meet their obligations to retirees.

IV. Global Forces: how we get to solutions

A. Everyone today holds a part of the solution to these issues. By our lifestyle choices, the comments we make to friends, the people we vote for, the letters we write, we all make choices.

B. The issues I am talking about require both national and global solutions — i.e., international collaboration of some kind is involved — and these global solutions involve behavioral change. The solutions are going to be slow and arduous. Neither of these are particularly popular messages.

C. We must work on the common wisdom that problems are global, behavioral, and long term but need to be worked on urgently. The example of population shows that success can result from a major and extended effort.

D. We must stand up for the common good and try to protect against the stridency of the activists and their captive media.

E. We need to continue to build the international system, perhaps with new forms of organization.

F. We need to use all of our powers of persuasion to avoid 'The Culture of Contentment', compellingly described by John Kenneth Galbraith. If we create societies in which the satisfied, cared–for middle class commands enough of a political majority that politicians are directed to their demands, rather than the kind of social investment that forestalls a build-up of future problems, the next millennium will hold more problems than promise.

G. We need to try to grow societies that have a little more patience for complicated answers and to escape from the world of the twenty-second sound byte, the answer by news clip, etc. That above all can destroy us. If we can expand our attention span, following the aforementioned course of action will help.

H. And we must celebrate our achievements — that's absolutely essential. And now I say — on with the challenges.

References

This discussion was based on a large part of the following sources:

Bongaarts, John. 1994. 'Population Policy Options in the Developing World,' *Science*, 11 February 1994, Vol. 263, pp. 771-776.

Bongaarts, John and Judith Bruce. 1995. 'The Cause of the Unmet Need for Contraception and the Social Content of Services,' *Studies in Family Planning* 26, no.2: 57-75.

Bongaarts, John and Sajeda Amin. 1997. 'Prospect for Fertility and Implications for Population Growth in South Asia,' Research Division Working Paper #94. New York: Population Council.

Brockerhoff, Martin and Ellen Brennan. 'The Poverty of Cities in the Developing World,' Policy Research Working Paper #96. New York: Population Council.

'Food: Enough for All,' *The Earth Times*. September 1-15, 1998:2.

Human Development Report 1997. United Nations Development Program. New York: Oxford University Press, 1997.

Human Development Report 1997. United Nations Development Program. New York: Oxford University Press, 1996.

Making a World of Difference – Celebrating 30 Years of Development Progress. United States Agency for International Development. Washington, DC: USAID 1998.

McNicoll, Geoffrey. 1997. 'Population and Poverty: A Review and Restatement,' Research Division Working Paper #105. New York: Population Council.

Population Growth and Our Caring Capacity. 1994 Population Council Issues Papers. New York: Population Council.

Sewell, John. 'The Changing Definition of Development and Development Cooperation,' Overseas Development Council. Prepared for a panel discussion at USAID's Conference on the 30th Anniversary of Tidewater, June 29, 1998, Washington, DC.

The Progress of Nations 1997. United Nations Children's Fund. New York: UNICEF, 1997.

The Unfinished Transition 1994. Population Council Issues Papers. New York: Population Council.

Todaro, Micheal P. 1997. 'Urbanization, Unemployment, and Migration in Africa: Theory and Policy,' Policy Research Division Working Paper #104. New York: Population Council.

'Roundup,' *The World Paper*, July/August 1998, p.10.

World Bank, *World Bank Development report, 1993.*

Barbara Herz and Shahidu P. Khandker, eds. *Women's Work, Education and Family Welfare in Peru,* World Bank, Discussion Papers #161, 1991.

Lawrence Summers, 'The Most Influential Investment,' *Scientific American,* August, 1992, page 132.

Christopher Coldough with Keith M. Lewin, *Educating All the Children,* Oxford University Press, 1993.

Elizabeth M. King and M. Anne Hill, eds. *Women's Education in Developing Countries: Barriers, Benefits, and Policies,* World Bank, 1992.

T. Paul Schulz, 'Investments in the Schooling and Health of Women and Men,' *Journal of Human Resources,* Fall 1993.

Population Action International, 'Closing the Gender Gap: Educating Girls,' *1993 Report on Progress Toward World Population Stablization.*

UNESCO, *World Education Report, 1993.*

Brady, Martha 'Laying the Foundation for Girls' Health Futures: Can Sports play a Role?' *Studies in Family Planning,* Vol 29, March 1998. The Population Council.

THE HONOURABLE
BARBARA J. MCDOUGALL

Barbara McDougall was a Member of Parliament for nine years, during which time she held several cabinet posts, including Finance, Employment and Immigration, and External Affairs. She is a graduate of the University of Toronto, is a Chartered Financial Analyst and has an honorary doctorate from St. Lawrence University.

Her extensive knowledge and expertise in international relations have led her to sit as a Canadian representative to the Inter-American Dialogue in Washington, the International Crisis Group in Brussels, and the International Advisory Board for the Council on Foreign Relations in New York.

Barbara McDougall was also a governor of the Toronto Stock Exchange and York University and has served as a director of several Canadian corporations and organizations, including the Bank of Nova Scotia, Corel, Stelco, the Canadian Opera Company and the Council for Canadian Unity. She served as President and CEO of the CIIA from 1998 to 2003. She is an Officer of the Order of Canada.

This paper was first presented as the 1999 Queen-Hughes Lecture.

The 1999 Queen-Hughes Lecture

Sovereignty: Not What It Used To Be

by Barbara McDougall

CANADIANS ARE AWARE THAT Winnipeg has played a prominent role in the history of Canada. Those of us here are also aware of Winnipeg's prominent role in the history of the Canadian Institute of International Affairs. This was the largest of the original 1928 branches and one of Canada's most active branches during the Thirties.

John Dafoe, the editor of the *Winnipeg Free Press*, became president of the national organization. Edgar J. Tarr, a city businessman, also served as president during the Thirties and led the CIIA delegation to the British Commonwealth Relations Conference in 1938.

One of the striking features of the early Winnipeg days was the preponderance of business people who were actively engaged in the founding of the branch, in its early leadership, and its development. Clearly, those visionary leaders saw the importance of international forces, no doubt for the success of their own commerce, but also for the broader community. They set a shining example for our business leaders of today.

Winnipeg is also known as a centre of lively intellectual debate, so it is also a good venue in which to open a discussion challenging some of our traditional views of sovereignty. In the early days of the Winnipeg chapter, in 1931, the Statute of Westminster bestowed on Canada for the first time 'sovereignty' in the field of foreign policy.

In those days, views on sovereignty had not changed for four hundred years: sovereignty was about borders, and the primacy of the state within those borders. Sovereignty was secured by military power, which if strong enough, could extend the sovereignty of one country to incorporate other countries in far-flung corners of the world: think of the British Empire.

139

Today that definition is no longer adequate. Many countries are struggling to redefine some of the traditional foreign policy concepts around sovereignty; certainly Canada is. And what better organization than the CIIA to help shape this discussion?

That's the reason I was delighted to become the president of such a venerable institution. I am a strong believer that the CIIA, with its interested and informed membership across the country, has a vital role to play in the shaping of public opinion, as many of our traditions in the field of international relations are being challenged.

That's the reason, as well, that the recent series of foreign policy consultations held by many CIIA branches across the country is so timely.

You will be aware from your own successful consultation here that many Canadians are taking a very thoughtful approach to what our foreign policy should be in the next century. Discussions have also been held in Victoria, Saskatoon, Ottawa and Toronto, with consultations yet to come in Montreal and Halifax. The results will be distilled into a report to our sponsoring organization, the Canadian Centre for Foreign Policy Development in the Department of Foreign Affairs, and naturally, to the minister. It will, of course, be made public.

Your consultations, like the others, had a good starting point: the excellent paper prepared by our former distinguished undersecretary, Si Taylor. Si's paper was not focused on sovereignty, but on three main themes: peace and security, prosperity and economic relations, and society and culture. I couldn't help noticing, however, that all these themes touch on sovereignty, and affect our views of sovereignty.

It seems trite to point out that in the field of foreign policy, as elsewhere, the speed of change, and its unpredictability, are constants. When I was appointed Secretary of State for External Affairs (as it was then called) in 1991, 1 was given several of those giant briefing books that bureaucrats are uniquely capable of producing and take a perverse pleasure in dumping on the desk of every new minister. One volume alone would take most of the minister's first month to digest, assuming she had nothing else to do.

Looking at the table of contents of my first briefing books at External Affairs today would tell an interesting story of how the world has turned upside down in those mere eight years. Through most of 1991 we were still thinking in very traditional terms about sovereignty and state or national security. Our concerns were bipolar in nature, focused on a Soviet Union that, while five years down Gorbachev's perestroika path, was still viewed as the main threat to Western security.

That Christmas, the Soviet Union collapsed. In fact, you will recall, President Gorbachev resigned precisely on Christmas Day. I think it was his final revenge on the outside world, ensuring that diplomats and ministers — even heads of government — would be called away from their Christmas turkey to design an appropriate response. That collapse spawned fifteen republics, and the Cold War was, to all intents and purposes, over. Realism tried to tell us that the process of converting Russia to a democratic society with a stable market economy would not be a short one. Nevertheless, we were swept up in a wave of optimism at the triumph of democracy and the rise of free and open markets. We were confident that the threat of nuclear attack, and Russian interference in the four corners of the world, would come to an end.

What we didn't anticipate though was, first of all, how long it would take to rout out the deeper vestiges of the Cold War, downsizing the military, disarming thousands of missiles, converting armament industries to more productive ends. And second, was the emergence of a whole host of new problems that have left us with an equally complex, dangerous and unpredictable world and a lack of coherent structures to deal with it.

To mention just a few of these: first, problems in the Balkans have further highlighted the Europeans' failure, despite numerous attempts, to institutionalize their security and defence initiative. In addition, Europe's declining military capabilities are highlighted by disagreements over policy, inadequate regional security and defence institutions and cuts to military budgets. It's not an exaggeration to say that the Europeans infuriate American legislators, who are looking to them to accept a greater share of the military burden.

Second, the abrupt expansion of the nuclear club to include India and Pakistan means that renewed efforts will have to be made to prevent further proliferation. The need for aggressive deterrence, thought to be on the wane, will have to remain a key strategy for the U.S. military on several grounds, including the not insignificant residual Russian threat, given the country's political and social instability, and China's nuclear capability. Both in Asia and in Europe though, sensitive deployments of nuclear armed missiles and the question of 'no first use' are issues which will be on the international agenda in the months ahead.

Third is the new whipping post for all things gone wrong in the world: globalization. We have been forcefully reminded through the Asian financial crisis of the threat to sovereignty that follows when technology opens our economies to sudden vast and unmanageable currency flows.

Technology can also lead to significant tax avoidance. It threatens our privacy, and some would say our culture. It allows money laundering on a scale never before contemplated: Britain recently disclosed that the largest foreign property investor in the United Kingdom is the Russian mafia.

We must not lose sight of the fact that globalization has led to immensely positive outcomes: the best surgeon in the world can now lecture at a medical school half way round the world given even modest technological resources. Economic integration and trade liberalization have brought increased prosperity to many countries, and may be able to transform others still lagging behind.

Still, this world as I've described it here bears almost no resemblance to the world that was described in my briefing books those few years ago. Today, we are attempting to recast some of our definitions of sovereignty and security in the light of new and different threats — or, in some cases, the old threats disguised in new clothing.

In Europe, the clash of those two long-held principles — the right to self-determination and the sanctity of borders — has led to intrastate conflict, political fragmentation, and ethno-nationalism: all old definitions. The old solution would have been to do nothing, to rely on the traditional shibboleth: that's an internal matter and there is nothing we can do. Instead, the NATO nations determined that the old ways did not hold, and that a state cannot be allowed to menace a whole underclass, at least, not in Europe. [Czech Republic President] Vaclev Havel, when speaking to the Canadian parliament last week, referred to the NATO campaign as "the first moral war". Is he right? Is this the better solution? In my view, NATO's exercise does have a moral purpose, and its response to Yugoslav aggression was the right one. Perhaps it is too soon to know whether we've chosen the right path. But we are right to recognize that new times may well call for new solutions.

When I was in Ottawa, we struggled with issues surrounding Canada's role in defending human rights: following a bloody attack by the Indonesian military in East Timor, we attempted unsuccessfully to build multilateral support for an appropriately severe response. Today, one of the government's primary foreign policy goals is to emphasize 'human security'.

This is essentially an interventionist philosophy that puts individual freedoms ahead of state supremacy and calls for international action in support of freedom of speech, freedom of worship, freedom from want, and freedom from fear. It is behind our initiatives in the areas of de-mining, small arms controls, and no first use of nuclear weapons. It underscores our concerns for environmental security, for the destruction of rain forests and the wasteful exploitation of clean resources.

It reinforces our search for common security through membership in organizations like the United Nations, NATO and NORAD, and it provides the rationale for the decision to move from peacekeeping to peacemaking. It is a logical enough step from state or national security to human security, but it is very difficult to bring them together in practice.

For one thing, a human security agenda requires a much more intrusive approach by the international community. Since 1949, Canada and other countries have been brought together in more and more multilateral organizations, and have signed more and more treaties, from the Columbia River Treaty to a ban on biological and chemical weapons. Every treaty we sign, every organization we join, diminishes our sovereignty — or perhaps a better term is 'alters our sovereignty' — at least incrementally — in anticipation of a greater good.

The shift to a human security agenda challenges our understanding of sovereignty quite radically. No longer does an abuser's sovereignty shield him if he is abusing his citizens. The old response: "That is an internal matter," has less currency. Today the answer is that human rights transcend borders. Augusto Pinochet found that out in the United Kingdom.

In the long run, an international consensus is essential to the successful implementation of a human security agenda. When the international community acts as one in these circumstances, it is called a humanitarian intervention; a country acting alone (especially a middle power) may well be doomed to failure.

Canada has always been an intrusive, some might say, meddlesome country. We have a high regard for the values we aspire to and we expect others to make the effort to emulate us. Many other countries appreciate our high principles and our unstinting work for good causes, and give us their support for membership on the UN Security Council. However, the Permanent-5 on that same Security Council, or fellow members of the G–7, are more likely to be irritated.

We used to 'put our money where our mouth is' in our campaign for human security, but the war against the deficit at home appears to have made a victim of our cause abroad. Canada's international capacity has been in decline now for more than five years, and was stretched for several years before that.

If Canada is serious about contributing to global security it cannot continue to scrimp and save on the backs of its military establishment. If it is serious about contributing to human security, it cannot continue to shrink the share of its GNP that it commits to overseas development assistance. If it is serious about the diplomatic role it says it wants to play, or the economic benefits it seeks from international trade, it cannot continue to short change the foreign service that is our front line in the fight for our global interests.

And interests, indeed, must remain a significant part of our international agenda, including our economic interests — or to continue the parallel — our economic security.

I would make the case that our economic sovereignty and security (not always the same thing, by the way) are as important as human security in looking at our foreign policy objectives. Consider the downfall of the so-called Asian tigers. Who would have thought, for example, in the heady year of 1991 — the year of my briefing books — that the tiger economies, with their year-over-year double-digit growth rates, would come unstuck in such devastating fashion? Touted as the engine of growth in the world economy, their collapse has shaken the faith of their citizens in open markets, and nearly brought down their all-too-shallow democracies, to say nothing of wreaking havoc in far-away Latin America.

The weakness in Japan, which accounts for seventy-five per cent of the combined Asia-Pacific economies, is even more troublesome. Japan's economic strength (and its security relationship with the United States) ensured stability throughout much of Asia. Its inability to generate growth in the region undermines the raison d'etre for its power and prestige. Does this augur the beginning of a major power shift towards China? Once again, the road ahead is not clear, nor should it not be ignored that China has economic problems of its own.

Economic and trade relations have important political implications, and not just in Asia. Sovereignty is affected by how governments determine their economic relationships — access to markets, controls on financial flows, technical assistance, regulatory regimes matter a great deal.

International financial institutions, in this context, are now key players in the resolution of economic problems. It is not the Commonwealth, or the United Nations, or NATO to which countries with economic difficulties turn. It is to the IMF, the World Bank, the Paris Club, or regional development banks. And it is membership on the boards of those institutions which gives countries economic power. That these organizations have economic power, rightly or wrongly, is a given. What is increasingly apparent, however, is that the actions of the institutions have political and hence security implications, thus crowding our sovereignty.

There is another economic player of great importance which cannot be ignored in this discussion of sovereignty, and that is business. The power of financially strong companies is not new: the "Governor and Company of Adventurers of England tradeing into the Hudson's Bay" being a local case in point. But it is not unusual today that many companies have more assets than middle-sized countries. And Coca-Cola even has its own department of diplomatic affairs to stick-handle its government relationships in countries where it does business. The significance of the nation state in defining security and defending sovereignty will clearly diminish, given the proliferation of economically powerful players.

So where does this leave us at the end of what Sir Thomas Beecham once called "this silly, savage and senseless" century? Well, if we choose to put human security first, how much are we willing to sacrifice other domestic interests to advance our values internationally? Almost everything we do outside our borders today presents us with a choice. How do we fit trade with China into our concerns for human rights abuse in that country? How far do we push our nuclear disarmament agenda in the faces of our G–7 partners, when we need their support on other issues? In a competitive and high risk setting, Canada needs not only to be a leader to achieve its ends, it needs to accommodate its friends and allies in working towards the most appropriate and effective policies to achieve its human security goals.

I would also challenge the government to put more emphasis on economic, as well as human security, and to encourage more thoughtful public discussion. By thoughtful public discussion I do not mean damning all corporations, short-term capital flows and private wealth — an updated, internationalized version of the old attack on corporate welfare bums. I mean looking at the globalized world we find ourselves in and harnessing its trends to do the most good for the most people.

Sylvia Ostry (another Winnipegger) pointed out recently that transparent, rules-based economic relationships will always be to Canada's advantage. In the so-called millennium round of trade talks now getting started under the WTO, Canada has an opportunity to conduct an excellent public discussion on economic security, its implications for sovereignty, and how best to achieve our security and sovereignty goals in the economic context. And what better organization to lead the discussion than the CIIA?!

And while I'm in the mode of giving the government advice, I'd like to offer the CIIA as the vehicle for another public discussion on the topic that is most on everyone's mind today: Kosovo. Not on whether or not the NATO action is right or wrong, but on the aftermath of the hostilities. In European capitals, talks are already quietly underway to develop a postwar action plan, including potential integration of the Balkans into European institutions.

Our government could invite a selected group of Canadians to prepare "concept papers" on the main issues: security for returning refugees, immediate rebuilding of the infrastructure in both Kosovo and Serbia, long-term development, and the formulation of democratic institutions. Our organization could then conduct the appropriate public discussion which would result in an effective Canadian response — with the collateral benefit of leading to a better-informed Canadian public.

The ongoing revolution in communications technology may have brought the suffering of Kosovo live and in technicolour into our living rooms every moment of every day, but it has not necessarily led to the better-informed public I am advocating.

Equally, there is a need in Canada to ensure that the values the country is pursuing reflects the thinking of Canadians across the country. With this need in mind, I believe that Canada needs the institute and that the CIIA needs more than ever to be an active participant in the formulation of foreign policy on a continuing basis.

There is a theory that in an age of 'down-sized' government — in all countries — think tanks like ours will become more important. Despite radically changed definitions of sovereignty, in a democracy, the broad public interest is still best defended by government. In a democracy, only government can claim to speak for the entire public. Think tanks like the CIIA give governments an excellent resource to inform the public, reflect the public, and bring together the widest possible diversity of expertise on a variety of complex issues without adding to the overhead, so to speak.

Exciting times lie ahead for the CIIA as we attempt to do more of what we do best. I hope you'll join in our efforts.

Sovereignty: Not What It Used To Be

Peter St. John

Peter St. John (pronounced Sin-jun) taught International Relations at the University of Manitoba for thirty-five years, retiring in 1998. Since his retirement, he has continued to teach, not only at the U of M, but also at the U.S. Airforce Special Operations School, the University of Winnipeg, the University of Victoria and St. Andrew's University in Scotland.

For the past twenty years, he has specialized in Intelligence, Espionage, Insurgency and Terrorism and developed the first course on these subjects in North America. He also taught Middle Eastern Politics and Canadian Foreign Policy.

In 1996, he won a University of Manitoba Outreach award and in 1997 the Stanton Award for Excellence in Teaching.

He is the author of *Air Piracy, Airport Security and International Terrorism* (1991) and has consulted widely for governments in North America. He also speaks regularly on radio and television, as well as to audiences across Canada and the United States.

He is married to writer and publisher Barbara Huck and together they have six daughters and two sons, as well as a passel of grandchildren. In 1998, Peter became the 9th Earl of Orkney.

This paper was given as the 2002 Queen-Hughes Lecture.

The 2002 Queen-Hughes Lecture

Nine-Eleven and the Islamic Fundamentalist Terrorist Mindset

by Peter St. John

In 1917, my father served in the Mesopotamian Campaign, fighting for the British forces with the Arabs against the Germans and the Turks in the First World War. That year, Kut al Amara, which is east of Baghdad, changed hands thirteen times in eleven months amid ferocious fighting. Finally, the Germans and Turks surrendered and my father was chosen to go out into no-man's land, meet a Turkish officer of equivalent rank, and exchange surrender terms. With white flags fluttering to indicate the truce and the opposing armies lined up and watching, the two men picked their way through the dead bodies toward the meeting point.

Suddenly a shot rang out and a bullet clipped my father's ear. He strode on. Another shot hit the dust at his feet; a third nipped his pant leg. In all, he walked through six shots en route to meeting the Turkish officer. Why didn't he duck or run for cover as I would have done? I asked him once and his answer was this: He was a soldier of the Royal Scots and the men of the Black Watch were standing in the ranks behind him, watching his progress. "Damned if I was going to back off in front of those guys," he told me. "The Royal Scots [often called 'Pilate's Bodyguard'] are the oldest regiment in the U.K., but the Black Watch *think* they are."

The next day, when the two officers exchanged the signed surrender papers, the Turk apologized to my father. "Sorry about that, old chap," he said, and explained that a Muslim Marsh Arab had recently joined the Arab forces. Seeing an infidel alone, in easy target range, he thought that if he could only kill him he would go straight to Heaven and have seventy maidens catering to his every need. "It's all right," the Turkish officer said apologetically, "his superior officer bayoneted him six times, one for each shot, and hung him up on a post as an example to others about what the white flag means."

The moral of this story is that violent Islamist behaviour is nothing new. In fact, as is the case with Christianity, it is as old as the religion itself. Islamic fundamentalist terrorism was around in 1917 and long before. I guess I am fortunate to be here to write this.

In this time of upheaval, uncertainty and terrorism in the wake of 9/11, it is extremely important to know who flew those planes into the World Trade Center towers and the Pentagon and why? In short, who is our enemy in today's war on terrorism?

The Origins of the Mindset

In September 1090 A.D., a man called Hassan Sabah seized a rocky fortress called Alamut, or the 'Eagle's Nest', northwest of Tehran in Persia, today's Iran. There Sabah, who became known as 'Lord of the Mountain', created a religious Islamic revolutionary movement. It aimed to purify the faith, which had been sullied by the unrighteous behaviour of the sultan of the Seljuk Empire, which was then ruling Persia. The movement was organized around Murshids, or 'guides', who were sent to study the word of Allah; Dais, or 'missionaries', who were to go out and propagate the word of God, and Fedayeen, or 'freedom fighters', who were to sacrifice themselves by killing for Allah, often using a poison dagger. This new doctrine of religious military order soon had a huge impact on the Empire; it led to the Ismaili sect of Islam, which terrorized both the Muslim and Christian worlds for more than 200 years.

In a short time, there was a string of forts through the remote regions of the Seljuk Empire, serving as a state within a state: 'The City of Faith existing side by side with the City of War.' Sound familiar by any chance? Fedayeen killed the Crusaders, and attacked the sultan; hundreds were executed, thousands died. The followers of Hassan Sabah were said to have gained their courage from mixing wine and opium. And so, the term Hashasheen or 'Smokers of Hash' was applied to Hassan's followers. The term evolved and they ended up being called 'The Assassins'. They certainly used political assassination in their war on their enemies — apostate members of their own religion as well as infidels.

But we are getting ahead of the story here, because it was not the Assassins who invented political murder, the Kharejites (as we shall see) did. Nevertheless, it was Hassan who developed political murder from an earlier doctrine as an important element in a coherent theory of political power. The lessons he taught were never forgotten in parts of the Islamic world; in fact, today they are attracting more disciples than ever.

The Kharejites emerged in the seventh century from the struggle for succession concerning the first four caliphs of the Muslim Empire. In Caliph Ali's camp were the zealots who decided that conflict over the Prophet's successor should not be put in human hands. Sovereignty came from God, not human discretion and because of their separation from discussion and pursuit of a bloody war of succession, these Kharejites became known in Islamic history as 'those who go out'. Three of four caliphs who succeeded the Prophet were assassinated by those who considered them to be 'weeds in the Garden of God'. Once a weed is clearly recognized as an enemy of the Faith, he becomes *mahdur-adamm* — 'one whose blood must be shed'. (In 1981, Anwar Sadat was assassinated because he was deemed to have become a weed in the Garden of God.)

Omar ibn Khattab, the second caliph, died of a poison dagger; Ottmar ibn Affan was murdered in 656 and in 661 the fourth caliph, Ali, was murdered giving rise to the Shiites. Ali was their first Imam. Shiite means 'partisan' in Arabic and refers to the partisans of Ali, the son-in-law of the Prophet, whom the Shiites consider should have succeeded the Prophet, not Abu Bkr, the first caliph.

According to the Shiites, the caliph should mete out divine justice, thus government by the Imam must be chaste. According to Amir Taheri, the Party of Allah was to use Islamic Jihad, or "violence and terror to convert by force, if necessary, all mankind to the faith of Muhammad." Thus 'Islamic terrorism' is a phenomenon, much like the Inquisition, and each of these is only a part of Islam and Christianity respectively. Jihad or 'holy war' is principally understood by the majority of followers of Islam as a struggle against evil within each individual believer. Thus fasting and intensification of prayer at Ramadan is a spiritual exercise. But, as we have seen, a minority has viewed Jihad as a duty of Muslims to resist the forces they consider to be conspiring against Islam. This means a physical struggle against the infidel, which in today's world means Western nations. In their book, *The Age of Sacred Terror*, authors Steven Simon and Daniel Benjamin speak of a thirteenth-century scholar by the name of ibn Tamiyyah, who lived on the edge of the Islamic empire. Ibn Tamiyyah's people were attacked by fellow Muslims, though of a different nationality, and as a theologian, he was deeply affected by the experience. As a result, he wrote that the Muslim has the right, indeed the duty, to attack not only the apostates within, but the infidel enemy without. Today, Osama bin Laden bases his attacks on the West, at least in part, on the writings of ibn Tamiyyah. According to the literate Muslim observer and writer Amir Taheri:

"Islamic terrorism has played a constant and key role in the revivalist movements in the Muslim world during the past 150 years. And, despite vehement protests from Westernized, Muslim intellectuals, the idea of murdering, maiming and menacing the enemy for the purpose of hastening the final triumph of Islam, has always held a very strong appeal among the Muslim masses."

So 'the enemy' today comes from a violent minority in both the Sunni and Shiite streams of Islam, from those who believe that assassination, political murder, suicide bombing and mass murder with weapons of mass destruction are needed and justified in implementing the Will of Allah today — particularly against the West. Call them radicals, or Islamists, or revolutionaries, these "Fundamentalists are terrorized by their vision of the contemporary world," writes Taheri. "They seek safety and protection in a past that did not exist as they imagine it today. Fear of life makes them worship death. They long to return to the womb of history, where they hope to feel warm once more in a cold world."

Hassan al Banna and the Muslim Brotherhood

The Islamic fundamentalist mindset was developed in Sunni and Shiite alike through two major episodes of the twentieth century. The first came in 1928 when Sheikh Hassan al-Banna of Egypt became founder and leader of the Ikhwan al-Moslemeen or Muslim Brotherhood. Central to the Brothers' philosophy was *tagiha* or 'the keeping of intents secret'. It involved the dagger, poison, the revolver and ... terrorism. These were to be the weapons of Islam against its enemies. By 1938, Hassan became the supreme guide of the movement and had declared war on the infidel — in this case the British. The Brothers by this time had a half-million members and two million sympathizers. They commenced a reign of terror in Egypt that was later to be the model for Iran and Lebanon. In January 1949, al-Banna was killed and in 1954, Premier (and later President) Gamal Abdul Nasser dismantled the Brothers, arresting thousands of them. But this did not prevent Sayyed Qutb, a noted hard-line leader of the movement and disciple of al-Banna, from inspiring further militants in the 1960s with his prison writings. He preached a personal Jihad against the apostate and Muslim enemies. By 1964, the movement was again a threat and in the repression of 1965 hundreds died. Qutb died a martyr or *shaheed* and out of this death down the road emerged Gamaat al-Islamiyya, the terrorist movement now in league with bin Laden's al Qaeda. Its leader Ayman al-Zawahiri was No. 2 to bin Laden. Islamic fundamentalist terrorism was reborn in Egypt and in the Sunni world by al-Ickhwan and today Palestinian martyrs committing suicide in order to kill the Jewish enemy are known as Shaheeds.

Ayatollah Khomeini and the Iranian Revolution (1979)

If one foot of terrorism fell in Egypt, in the Sunni community, the other foot fell in Iran, among the Shiite followers of Ayatollah Ruholla Khomeini. One of Khomeini's first acts, according to Taheri who was, after all, editor of *The Iranian Times*, was to create the Hizb-Allah, or Party of God, which consisted of young people. For three years youths would join the Hizballah and wait expectantly for the call to be a suicide volunteer. If chosen, they would take it as a sign of Allah's favour and if they did achieve their mission, they would be called *enteharis*, the Shiite name for suicide bomber or 'Martyr for God'. As an extension of this principle, Khomeini had nine- to twelve-year-old children walk out into the Iraqi minefields in the Iraq-Iran war, to sacrifice their bodies so that the Iranian armies could invade. The families of those who died in this manner were paid $150 per child. Later, Iranian religiously-inspired shock troops, the Red Guards, would cross over into Syria to the Bekaa Valley where they helped to create today's Hizballah.

The Afghan Jihad against the U.S.S.R. (1979)

In retrospect, the Afghan Jihad can be seen as the catalyst that brought together Sunni and Shiite radicals — traditional enemies — and coalesced them into the al Queda movement under the leadership of Osama bin Laden. It was a fateful melding of the forces of modern terrorism. Too bad the Russians committed to such a war. For the Ickhwan in Saudi Arabia the war was a huge opportunity to spread their austere, puritanical doctrine of Wahhabism. Under the banner of Deobandism, Saudi fundamentalists developed hundreds of radical Sunni religious schools, which taught intolerance and violence in Peshawar, Quetta and the Northwest frontier of Pakistan. They spread into Kashmir and were an inspiration for the Taliban regime in Afghanistan. The Saudis put at least $3 billion into these efforts, while the CIA for their part put $3 billion into arming the Afghan militants who fought the Russians, Stinger missiles and all! Ahmed Rashid has written about all this in his book *Taliban*.

In the middle of all this fighting a young fundraiser and millionaire from Saudi Arabia was seen visiting wounded soldiers in hospital, building roads, and even on occasion, joining in battle. This is where the legend of bin Laden starts and he is credited with attracting between 70,000 and 80,000 Arab Muslims to come and fight in the Afghan Jihad. They were Muslims from every country of the Arab world, and once the Soviets were ejected, these battle-hardened guerrillas went back to fight in similar wars for Islamic governments in Algeria, Egypt, Chechnya and Bosnia. Bin Laden has a lot to answer for in today's religious, terrorist violence.

Meanwhile, he married into the family of Mullah Omar, the leader of the Taliban. Prior to this period, bin Laden seems to have undergone a conversion experience. As a young man he had frequented nightclubs in Beirut and lived a carefree life of luxury. His father, who was from Yemen, had made millions rebuilding the mosque at Mecca and building roads in Saudi Arabia. Things changed when his father died, though whether he died in an air crash or committed suicide is not certain, for bin Laden recalled his father's wish that one of his children would do something significant for Islam. Over a period of years, he emerged as the reconciler of radical Islamic factions, the creator of 'The Base' or al Qaeda, and the builder of a virtual state of terrorists capable of striking at the very heart of America — 9/11. Much more could be said about all this, but there is only time here to draw attention to bin Laden's role in catalyzing the forces of anti-Westernism and nurturing a significant radical movement worldwide.

The Invasion of Lebanon by Israel (1982)

In 1982, the Israelis invaded Lebanon in order to end the Palestinian Liberation Organization's virtual occupation of the southern part of the country. I was there as the Israeli army rolled into Shiite southern Lebanon and embarked on a campaign of destruction. As their homes and communities were flattened, the significant Shiite minority moved north to the outskirts of Beirut, where they sheltered pathetically on the city's outer limits. Seeing an opportunity, Ayatollah Khomeini sent his Red Guards to the Bekaa Valley to train Shiite leaders; soon he had created one of the most dangerous terrorist groups in the world — Hizballah. Not long after, Hizballah signaled its emergence by killing 241 American Marines in a suicide bombing. Not only did this enrage the United States, it marked the beginning of the modern phase of suicide bombing. It's ironic, given the Israeli intent more than two decades ago, that today, as a result, suicide bombings are more common in Israel today than almost anywhere else in the world. What goes around comes around.

TWA 847 (1985) and Pan Am 103 (1988)

Islamic fundamentalist terrorism developed the expertise to hijack, bomb, and finally destroy planes through an evil genius by the name of Imad Mughnyah, who is still a leader of the violent wing of Hizballah. It was he who orchestrated the thirteen-day hijack of TWA 847, which moved between Athens, Beirut and Algiers. It was he who hijacked a Kuwait Air flight in 1988 with a member of the Kuwati royal family on board. And his expertise led to the 1988 bombing and destruction of Pan Am 103 over Lockerbie, Scotland, which resulted in 273 deaths.

It is my belief that Mughnyah was an instrument of the Ayatollah Khomeini, who orchestrated the Pan Am bombing. I also believe that Khomeini paid $10 million US to have Ahmed Jibril, leader of the Popular Front for the Liberation of Palestine, General Command (PFLP–GC), destroy the American commercial aircraft in revenge for the shooting down of an Iranian airbus full of pilgrims by the *USS Vincennes* earlier in 1988. The Americans had refused to accept any responsibility for the Iranian airbus incident and an enraged Khomeini had promised $10 million to anyone who would destroy an American flag carrier. Because the plot was discovered in Germany before it could be carried out, the plans had to be changed. The bomb travelled with Libyan help via Malta to Frankfurt and then London. No one should be under any illusion that Khomeini was not openly 'declaring war' on the U.S. and its allies in a way that was later to be emphasized, emulated and realized by bin Laden's 1998 Fatwa.

The al Nosair assassination of Meir Kahane (1990)

By now, most of the individual elements were in place for a suicide mission such as the 9/11 attack on the World Trade Center in New York. However, the location of an attack and how to accomplish it were yet not clear to bin Laden. In November 1990, a Palestinian killed Meir Kahane, the extremist leader of the Kach Movement in Israel, which was aimed at ridding that country of all Arabs. The imprisonment of al Nosair so enraged and mobilized the Muslim Afghani community in New York, that in 1992 Ramzi Youssef, the al Qaeda bomb maker, arrived in New York to help plan an attack on the World Trade Center. Such an attack would be both a declaration of war against the Jews of New York, and a lethal blow to the financial power of the United States, all in one fell swoop.

The First World Trade Center bombing (1993)

Working with an incredible bunch of incompetents, on February 26th, 1993, Ramzi Youssef managed to introduce a 1,500-pound bomb into a parking place at the bottom of one of the twin towers. Youssef's plan was that the two towers would implode, one against the other, and that with the addition of cyanide poisoning, 100,000 might be killed in downtown Manhattan! However, the parking space in which Youssef had planned to place the bomb was unavailable and the group's calculations were off. As the ill-fated, but nevertheless destructive explosion took place, Ramzi Youssef was winging his way back to Pakistan and on to the Philippines, where he was later to plan fresh infamy. Instead, Abdul Rahman, a blind Egyptian sheik and cleric, was put on trial for the bombing and imprisoned in the U.S. Abdul Rahman was an open member of Gamaa Islamiya and he had planned further attacks on the United Nations and the Hudson River tunnel. Unfortunately, Western intelligence sources had not yet learned that one of al Qaeda's quaint little habits was to get things right after they had gone wrong. In retrospect, it's clear they should have begun imagining how else the World Trade Center might be attacked! It might not have taken a great deal of imagination to come up with an alternative scenario. In 1991, in an interview on Good Morning America, I predicted that Islamic extremists would fly suicide planes into New York skyscrapers; at the time, I thought the targets might be the Chrysler Building or the Empire State Building, but that was before Ramzi Youssef's first attempt at the World Trade Center.

In 1995, Youssef was arrested in Pakistan after one of his bombs blew up in his Manila apartment, forcing a quick escape that left behind a computer full of dastardly plans. There, on the computer hard drive, was his scheme to simultaneously bomb as many as eleven U.S. commercial aircraft arriving from abroad. The scope and audacity of such an attack had the potential to create mass hysteria in the U.S. and might even have been more devastating than the 2001 attack on the World Trade Center.

Osama bin Laden and al Qaeda (1994-5)

By the end of the Gulf War in 1991, a rupture had developed between the moderates and the radicals in Saudi Arabia. The ruling conservative middle class had requested the presence of American troops, while the radical Wahhabis in opposition spat venom and pledged all-out war on the Crusader infidels of America. At the same time, bin Laden, who had returned from Afghanistan, was encouraging radicalization among the Saudis. Eventually, he was forced to leave Saudi Arabia; he spent several years in Sudan and ultimately, thanks to inept American diplomacy, returned to Afghanistan in 1996. By now, the final showdown was in sight, for throughout the 1990s, bin Laden had sought to unite the Saudi-Hizballah, Gamaa Islamiya in Egypt, the Taliban in Afghanistan and al Qaeda to create a great front of radical confrontation with the West. During the same period, bin Laden had hoped that the Islamic Mujahideen in Bosnia, Egypt and Algeria would triumph, but in all three nations they failed to establish a Muslim government.

Meanwhile, he had his followers swear an oath of allegiance to himself as Caliph of Islam. The Ottoman Caliphate had been abandoned in 1924 and bin Laden sees himself as the heir to that exalted spiritual and temporal leadership of the Muslim world. Ambitious indeed! In 1996 and 1998, this seventeenth of fifty-seven children was issuing 'Fatwas', which effectively declared war on behalf of the radical Islamic elements against all moderate (read corrupt and apostate) regimes of the Muslim and Arab world. He also declared war on Jews, Americans and Crusaders. Now bin Laden was fighting not only 'the near enemies' of his own world, but 'the far enemies' of the Western states. This reversed an historic commitment in Islam.

Khobar Towers (1996), The East African Embassies (1998) and the USS Cole (1999)

The End Game was clearly now in sight, with bin Laden attempting to rock the majoritarian, moderate Muslim boat until it capsized, provoking the intervention of God. This has often been the thinking of Millennialist religious fanatics — to provoke God to intervene.

The Khobar Towers bombing killed seventeen Americans and gained huge support for bin Laden in Saudi Arabia. Then on August 14, 1998, the American embassies in Nairobi, Kenya, and Dar es Salaam, Tanzania, were almost simultaneously bombed, killing 224 people and wounding 1,000. Just over a year later, in November 1999, the *USS Cole*, a symbol of American military power, was rammed by a suicide power boat while in port at Aden, causing multiple American deaths. Clearly, the American superpower was vulnerable.

All these were harbingers of a greater storm to come on September 11th, 2001 in New York and Washington. On that day, 3,000 died in the World Trade Center, 265 died in the four aircraft involved and 123 were killed in the Pentagon. In the eyes of militant Islam, a blow had been dealt the heart of American economic power and Jewish American influence.

The Interpretation and Conclusion

All that remains is to attempt to step into the minds of Islamic Fundamentalists and explain 9/11.

Like the great French scholar of fundamentalism, Gilles Keppel, I believe that 9/11 was a gigantic provocation. It was a blast calculated to restart the radical Islamist movement. Its principal objective? To mobilize the Muslim masses behind a victorious (and worldwide) Jihad. Such a Jihad would overthrow the corrupt Arab regimes, replacing them with pure Islamic states. And by ratcheting up the scale of attack, bin Laden hoped to create a Muslim vanguard that would kill Americans on American soil, and trigger an anticipated U.S. retaliation against the Taliban, which would lead to a massive cemetery for American troops, through another Afghan Jihad. Al Qaeda networks began a strategy of 'substitution' in which, by attacking highly symbolic and important economic targets, America could be brought to its knees.

Included in this strategy was an attempt to transfer the aspirations of the Jihad to the Palestinian Intifada: the American-supported Israeli regime would be seen as an abomination to all Arabs and Muslims and serve as a further cause for radicalizing the Muslim world. Unfortunately for bin Laden and fortunately for us, the big bang failed to move the Muslim masses and their clerics. But it has spawned a loose terrorist network of radical Islamic groups, which act as a virtual state in attacking Western interests. Further attacks since 9/11 have been seen in Saudi Arabia, Turkey, Bali, Indonesia, and the Madrid train bombings. Undoubtedly, there will be many more painful skirmishes in this war on terrorism, and the targets of these skirmishes will likely include Canada, which is, according to bin Laden, number five on the al Qaeda hit list. It's slightly unnerving to note that ours is the only country on the list that has not yet been attacked.

In the meantime, let's not harbour any illusions. The war on terrorism will be a long, hard-fought battle between intelligence agencies, counter-intelligence and counter-terrorism forces and special operations troops. As always, many innocents will be killed, as the radical elements worldwide are rooted out and put down by force. Since much of this war may be fought within the Western democracies, it is of crucial importance that ordinary, thoughtful citizens begin to understand the Islamic fundamentalist terrorist mindset. It is a spin-off of the age of sacred terror and, we can only hope, a precursor to massive, constructive and much-needed social and political change in the Islamic Arab world from Mauritania to Pakistan and beyond.

References

Bauer, Robert. *See No Evil.* Three Rivers Press, NY, 2002.

Benjamin, D and Simon, S. *The Age of Sacred Terror.* Random House, NY, 2002.

Bergen, Peter l. *Holy War, Inc.: Inside the Secret War of Osama bin Laden.* Free Press, NY, 2001.

Rashid, Ahmed, *Taliban: Militant Islam, Oil and Fundamentalism in Central Asia.* Yale University Press, London, 2001.

Taheri, Amir S. *Holy Terror: The Inside Story of Islamic Terrorism.* Sphere Books, London, 1987.

Sir Andrew Burns, KCMG

Born on 21 July 1943, Sir (Robert) Andrew Burns read Classics at Trinity College, Cambridge, joined the Diplomatic Service in 1965, and studied Urdu and Hindi at the School of Oriental and African Studies in London. His first foreign service post was in New Delhi in 1967.

During the years that followed, he served as desk officer for the Balkan countries, Head of Chancery at the British Embassy in Bucharest, visiting Fellow at the Harvard University's Center for International Affairs, before being appointed Counsellor at the British Embassy in Washington and Head of British Information Services in New York. Returning to London, he was first Head of South Asian Department (1986-88), then Head of News Department (1988-90) where as the official FCO spokesman he was also Press Secretary to three successive Foreign Secretaries.

In 1992 he was appointed British Ambassador to Israel, a posting that coincided with the second administration of Prime Minister Yitzhak Rabin. He returned to London in 1995 to be the Deputy Under Secretary of State responsible for the UK's bilateral relations outside Europe and for the UK's world-wide trade and investment promotion.

In November 1997, he was appointed British Consul General to the Special Administrative Region of Hong Kong, following the transfer of sovereignty to the People's Republic of China, and also to Macau.

Sir Andrew is married to Sarah Cadogan. They have two sons and a daughter. Lady Burns, who has been previously both a journalist and a personal financial adviser, is now a London Magistrate (Justice of the Peace).

This paper was presented to a joint meeting of the CIIA, the Intrepid Society, the English Speaking Union and the Commonwealth Society in 2003.

The 2003 Queen-Hughes Lecture

Iraq and the Implications for Canada

by Sir Andrew Burns

I WANT TO TALK ABOUT THE CONFLICT IN IRAQ and the implication it has for Canada's transatlantic relationship [with Britain]. My diplomatic career began in 1965 and I lived in Romania during the dark years of communism in the 1970s. For most of the years since I joined the Foreign Service the dominant international issue was the Cold War. Its end, in 1989, was an enormous relief and a justification of the success of the North Atlantic Alliance in standing firm against the menace and intrigues of communism, the Soviet Union and the Warsaw Pact.

I can remember watching television in Paris, with tears in my eyes, as the regime in Bucharest came to an end. No one wants to go back to those days. Instead we are seeing the countries of Central and Eastern Europe rejoining the community of European democracies, joining first NATO and then the European Union. Enlargement of the European Union [which took place in April 2003] will effectively mean that all the great cities and civilizations of Europe are now once again united.

And through all this time, a persistent theme has been our determined effort to constrain the spread of weapons of mass destruction: nuclear, biological and chemical. We have struggled to set up arrangements for international negotiation designed to ensure that differences between states would be resolved multilaterally and by peaceful means, rather than unilaterally by force of arms.

The Conference on Security and Cooperation in Europe, at which I was a negotiator for three years back in the 1970s, and in which Canada was a valued colleague, was a paradigm for the kind of multilateral negotiations by consensus that have created the hope of a lasting peace in Europe.

But as in all societies, keeping the peace means enforcing law and order. You hope to do this without violence, but at the end of the day the guaranteed threat of force is what deters the reckless or those with malice aforethought. The end of the Cold War and the spread of globalization have opened huge prospects of prosperity and peace to millions and millions of people around the world. But unfortunately, they have also facilitated terrorism and the settling of old scores. We see increasing examples of freelance, one might almost say privatized, violence. The natural instinct of all people around the world, to be able to bring up their families in peace and prosperity, is matched by the renewed assertions of parochial interests with scant regard for the safety of other groups or the broader security of the world.

The Middle East has been the cockpit for many conflicts over the ages. Two serve as a focus for modern minds.

The Arab-Israeli dispute

The first and perhaps most destructive has been the Arab-Israeli dispute. As a former Ambassador to Israel, I helped to nurture the tantalizing progress made in the Oslo Agreements. Since then the situation has become more violent and dangerous. What we are now working towards is the publication of what is called the Road Map, drawn up by a group known as the Quartet: the United States, Russia, the United Nations and the European Union. The hope is that this will chart a course to a just resolution of the dispute within a limited time, and will express the will of the international community with unprecedented force and clarity.

The broad outlines of a settlement have been known for many years. We need only look back at the key international statements of principle on the dispute since 1967: the UN Security Council Resolutions 242, 338 and 1397; the terms of reference drawn up at the Conference of Madrid; the principle of land for peace; the existing agreements between the two parties; and the tremendously important Arab League Initiative in March 2002, offering Israel full normalization of relations with its neighbours in the context of a settlement.

The objective, as I say, is crystal clear now. A State of Israel able to live at peace within secure and respected borders. And the establishment of a viable Palestinian state.

To have a viable Palestinian state you have to have a viable institution inside Palestine. That is why the British prime minister has been so vocal and active in encouraging the Palestinians to reform their own institutions. That is why the British foreign secretary chaired a meeting of Palestinian representatives in London this January. After a further meeting in February this led to the appointment of Palestinian Prime Minister Abu Mazen. Now Abu Mazen is about to appoint his cabinet. Once its members are approved by the Palestinian Legislative Council we can get on with the Road Map; improving the viability of the Palestinian State based on borders originally recognized in 1967; ensured security for Israel; an end to the settlements; a solution to the problem of refugees and a capital for the State of Palestine within Jerusalem.

We very strongly believe that the present hostility towards the West in the Islamic world is fuelled by anger at the persistent inability of the world to bring peace and reconciliation to the conflict between Israel and the Palestinians. The anger felt at the continuing violence in Israel and along the West Bank and Gaza explains why so much public opinion in the Middle East feels ambivalent towards the wicked acts of terrorism we have seen in recent times. That anger and frustration can never justify, rationalize or explain those criminal acts of terrorism. But if we are to deal with the terrorists we have to find a way of ensuring that we win the full-hearted support of moderate opinion.

Iraq

The other dangerous conflict is in Iraq. Over the past twelve years no government has worked harder than the British government to try and bring about the peaceful disarmament of Iraq as required by successive resolutions of the United Nations Security Council. It is deeply disappointing that the intensive negotiations over so many years failed to achieve a peaceful resolution.

We cannot ignore the clear, prolonged and universally available evidence that Iraq has repeatedly defied the United Nations by refusing to disarm its weapons of mass destruction. Under the terms of successive UN resolutions, Iraq has a duty to do this in full, active and genuine cooperation with the UN. But the express and explicit demands of the Security Council were never carried out by Iraq. And the UN never succeeded in drawing the right conclusions about the consequence of that defiance of the Security Council.

You will recall the history. Having already shown a cavalier disregard for his neighbours in the war Saddam Hussein provoked with Iran, which cost more than a million men, and for his own people through the use of chemical weapons to kill the inhabitants of the village of Halabja, Saddam Hussein invaded Kuwait in 1991. Aware of his long track record of brutality at home, UNSCR [UN Security Council Resolution] 678 authorized the use of force to push Saddam Hussein back out of Kuwait. After the war, UNSCR 687 ordered the disarmament of Iraq as a condition of the ceasefire. Any material breach of 687 automatically revives the authority to use force set out earlier in 678. In November, the unanimously approved UNSCR 1441 determined that despite repeated requests and pressure over the preceding ten years, Iraq was still continuing in material breach of that ceasefire resolution 687.

UNSCR 1441 gave Iraq "a final opportunity to comply with its disarmament obligations". It provided that if Iraq did not comply, then that would constitute a further material breach and that in that case, there would be serious consequences.

Saddam did not comply and therefore was in material breach of 1441. The original authority to use force in Resolution 678 was therefore revived. We made it amply clear that we would have preferred to have a second UN Resolution confirming the universal determination of the world that Iraq had stretched international patience too far.

Resolution 1441 was adopted unanimously but not, regrettably, implemented with any rigour by a united Council. Yet international peace and security cannot be responsibly maintained by avoiding hard decisions. Iraq was clearly determined, even in the face of the threat of military action, to hang on to its prohibited weapons, with all the risks that posed to peace and security in the region and more widely, including U.K. national security. Iraq has furthermore valued its defiance over the wellbeing of its own people, who have as a consequence endured a decade of debilitating sanctions.

We deeply regret the differences within the Security Council that have marked the past few months of discussion on this subject, but we came to the conclusion very reluctantly that the dangers of backing down in the face of Iraqi intransigence were greater than the dangers of going ahead. A broad coalition of well over forty states is now supporting U.K., U.S. and Australian action to enforce Security Council decisions. This action is being directed only at the regime in Baghdad. We have done everything possible to minimize the effect on civilians, to leave the infrastructure intact and to ensure that the necessary humanitarian assistance reaches the Iraqi people as quickly as possible.

Our immediate priority was to relaunch the Oil for Food programme, on which sixty per cent of Iraqis remain dependent. Of course we accept in full our obligations under international humanitarian law. The U.K. has committed approximately $541 million for humanitarian assistance in Iraq, with over half already allocated to the UN, the Red Cross and Red Crescent, and Non-Governmental Organizations. The U.K. is also contributing a fifth of the growing European Union contribution. Coalition engineers have been hard at work to build a water pipeline from Kuwait to Umm Qasr, now delivering two million litres of water a day. We are engaged in the distribution of supplies in southern Iraq, and have delivered two shiploads of emergency supplies.

Looking ahead, we are now considering the role which the UN can play in building a stable and prosperous Iraq. UN expertise, and that of all the international community, will be needed to achieve this. The U.K. is clear that the UN must take a central role in the future of Iraq. We want to see a well functioning Iraq that no longer presents a threat to international peace and security; where people can enjoy their fundamental rights without fear of oppression; where a representative government can provide effectively for its people and manage its natural resources for the benefit of all its population.

Iraq was once a cultural powerhouse, one of the most sophisticated countries in the Middle East. It has a highly-educated population and enormous natural resources. But the devastation in Iraq is a direct result of Saddam Hussein's misrule over a long period. Where he was in control, his overriding objective was to bolster the strength of his regime. Where he did not control the country, in the north of Iraq, the people have done rather better. But the challenge is huge, and one to which we look forward to working with many countries around the world, including Canada. Without a properly functioning Oil for Food program, Iraq could need $1 billion US per month in humanitarian aid alone. We welcome Canadian pledges. There is lots we can do together.

Working with Canada

Canada is one of the firmest and most reliable allies of the United Kingdom. We have been through a great deal together over the last century. We shall never forget the debt we owe you for the support you gave us in the two world wars.

We have been united too in the war on terrorism. We both recognize the very serious threat which our societies now face. We are both countries which are only too aware of the limitations of our own military capabilities. We know what we do, we do well. We often wish we could do much more. We know we have to work together.

We have been cooperating very closely in ensuring safe shipping in the Gulf as part of Operation Enduring Freedom. We have been working in strongly complementary ways in Afghanistan to bring peace and security back to that troubled country. Our forces work closely together in Bosnia. Our forces train very successfully in Alberta and Labrador.

Of course it was a pity that you decided you could not join the military campaign to enforce Resolution 1441. But I know that there are many ways in which we will continue to collaborate in trying to make the world a safer place. The habits of cooperation between us are deep and very practical. I am sure that we shall show the world their continuing effectiveness as we face up to the post conflict reconstruction challenge in Iraq and continue our world-wide battle with terrorism.

The UN, the EU and NATO

This latest conflict has produced dramatic strains within the North Atlantic Alliance and within the European Union. This is indeed very regrettable, but not a disaster. As successive communiqués from Brussels make plain: The EU is committed to the territorial integrity, the sovereignty, the political stability and the full effective disarmament of the Iraqi people, including all people belonging to minorities.

We believe that the UN must continue to play a central role during and after the current crisis. The UN system has a unique capacity and practical experience in coordinating assistance in post-conflict state. We believe the Security Council should give the United Nations a strong mandate for this mission. We urgently need to address the major humanitarian needs that will arise from the conflict. The EU wishes to be actively involved in this field in accordance with established principles.

We want to contribute effectively to the conditions allowing all Iraqis to live in freedom, dignity and prosperity under a representative government that will be at peace with its neighbours and an active member of the international community.

I don't think there is anybody in Europe who would disagree with those sentiments. I don't think there is anybody in Canada who would disagree with those sentiments. There is far more that unites us than disunites us. And it will be a tragedy if our own internal differences weaken us in our ability to protect our societies from the very serious threats of terrorism and weapons of mass destruction.

We know that the terrorist groups would like to get their hands on these weapons. That is one of the reasons why it has been so urgent to disarm a country like Iraq which has shown a disturbing readiness, not only to use these weapons, but to encourage terrorist groups.

Finally, there is a growing and deep fear in many quarters that the natural partnership between Europe and North America, which has served us all so well over the last fifty years, is becoming irrelevant in a unipolar world. There is an argument out there that the right way to respond to this U.S. dominance and strength is to establish some counterweight, some alternative power and of attraction, which could stand up to the Americans and assert other points of view.

The government I represent is deeply committed to making a success of the European Union, where the bulk of our economic interests lie. But we are equally adamantly opposed to the idea that partnership with the United States, and indeed with Canada, is no longer a priority. On the contrary, we believe that we must redouble our efforts to work with the United States in a way which will reestablish Western unity and thus allow us to play the strongly positive and constructive role we want to play in resolving world tensions — whether these be in the Middle East, or elsewhere, from the proliferation of weapons of mass destruction, from terrorism or from poverty.

COLIN ROBERTSON

Born in Winnipeg and educated at the University of Manitoba and the Norman Paterson School of International Affairs at Carleton, Colin Robertson has served as a diplomat and Canadian Consul for more than twenty-five years. His postings have included five years in Hong Kong and several stints in the United States, including assignments in New York and Washington as well as four years as Consul General in Los Angeles.

Returning to Ottawa between international postings, he served as Director General of Public Affairs for Treasury Board and Director General of Communications for the Department of Foreign Affairs. He is currently Minister (Advocacy) and Head of the Washington Secretariat at the Canadian Embassy.

Married to journalist and public relations specialist Maureen Boyd, Colin has three well-travelled children and an amiable golden retriever.

This paper was given at the University of Manitoba, in conjunction with Mr. Robertson's alumni award.

2004

Working With America After 9/11

by Colin Robertson

T ODAY WE LIVE IN what the French call the shadow of the 'hyperpower'. America is preponderant. As Colin Powell described it in a recent conversation with P.J. O'Rourke [in *The Atlantic Monthly*]:

> We are a superpower that cannot be touched in this generation by anyone in terms of military power, economic power, the strength of our political system and our values system. What we would like to see is a greater understanding of power, of the democratic system, the open market economic system, the rights of men and women to achieve their destiny as God has directed them to do if they are willing to work for it. And we really do not wish to go to war with people. But, by God, we will have the strongest military around. And that's not a bad thing to have. It encourages and champions our friends that are weak and it chills the ambitions of the evil.

Powell's assessment is reflective of American thinking. The rest of us have to come to terms with an America that is different since 9/11. James Q. Wilson, the American political philosopher, told me it is the most profound psychic shock to America since Pearl Harbour. For 9/11 revealed that America was vulnerable. In response, America has gone to war, first in Afghanistan and now in Iraq.

Canadians do not appreciate how profound a change 9/11 has made to Americans' sense of security (or should I say insecurity). Security concerns are never far from the surface and this is playing out in the current electoral campaign, especially in the presidential race. It manifests itself on four levels, all of which have implications for Canada:

• Economic security: no one feels better off than they did four years ago. Normally, this would work for the Democrats; it did in 1992 when Bill Clinton successfully exploited the issue against George Bush. John Kerry and John Edwards have sounded the claxon on 'outsourcing' and the 'export' of American jobs. Canadians need to be vigilant: nearly ninety per cent of our exports go south. Nearly half of our GDP is dependent on access to the American market.

• National security and the campaign against terrorism, coupled with growing unease over the conduct and outcome of the war in Iraq: the world is seen as an increasingly dangerous place for Americans. George W. Bush argues that it is better to take the battle to terrorists rather than let the terrorists come to America and he couples this with a heartfelt conviction that America and the free world have a responsibility, indeed a duty, to establish liberty and freedom, by force of arms if necessary. As he put it at the UN last week, "I have faith in the transforming power of freedom." And as he has also said, in the campaign against terrorism, "you are either with us or not." The challenges for Canada are obvious.

• Personal security at home, where no one feels safer than they did before 9/11: concern over personal security helps explain why the ban on sales of AK-47s and the like failed to be renewed, despite the urgings of people like Jim Brady, Ronald Reagan's press spokesman who was paralyzed in the assasination attempt on the president. *Bowling for Columbine*, Michael Moore's last film, is instructive on this count. It was less about the American fixation with the right to bear arms than the 'fear' culture. It's a culture reinforced daily by the media.

• Cultural security that manifests itself through the divide over support for gay marriage and abortion: geographically, it is expressed through the red and blue states. As one pundit put it, those in red states 'hunt', prey and execute, while in the blue they just 'play around'.

So how does Canada deal with a changed America in a dangerous world that lacks anchors and needs new governance? We start from the axiom, expressed by Lord Palmerston, that nations have "no permanent friends or enemies, only permanent interests."

Prosperity pays for those things that help define what is Canadian and our prosperity is dependent on our ability to trade. Nearly half of our GDP depends on trade. And our main trading partner is the United States. More than eighty per cent of our trade is destined for the United States: it's worth over a million dollars a minute. Most of it goes by truck: 1,500 cross the border each hour. And then there's the people flow: 300,000 cross back and forth daily.

The Canadian dilemma, even before Confederation, has always been how far to go with the United States. Geography and commerce draws us south. During the mid-nineteenth century, we enjoyed reciprocity with the United States. Then the American Civil War and imperial interests intervened and we recoiled.

Confederation was in part a response to America and the menace of 'manifest destiny'. National cohesion required us to defy market gravity and create bonds that stretched east and west. In trade, this meant a National Policy that gave preference to trade between provinces through the protection of manufacturing and eventually to supply marketing boards for wheat, pork, poultry and dairy products. Internationally, we tried to create counterweights to the United States, through trade arrangements with Britain and the Commonwealth under R.B. Bennett and later John Diefenbaker, then with Japan and Europe under Pierre Trudeau. But while you can take a horse to water, you can't make it drink.

In 1985, Brian Mulroney began negotiations for a comprehensive free trade agreement with the United States. It was an act of considerable political courage. Not only had he derided the idea in his leadership campaign, but traditional Conservative policy opposed free trade. And there was the political lesson of 1911 and the failure of an earlier Québec prime minister, Sir Wilfred Laurier. At the time negotiations began, only twenty-five per cent of Canadians supported the idea; more were opposed and most weren't sure why it was necessary. It was not the 'leap in the dark' that many critics described. Donald Macdonald had done the intellectual homework in the 150 volumes that comprised his enquiry into Canada's economic union and development prospects. Macdonald's work was probably the most valuable economic study since Rowell-Sirois.

By any measure free trade has been a success. Canada has always been a trading nation. Free trade has made us into a nation of traders. And with success. The economic prosperity of the past decade has been trade driven and that trade has grown mostly with the United States. Look at any of the indicators: interprovincial trade has been flat, but with the U.S. and, since NAFTA brought in Mexico, our trade has expanded sixfold.

Even the CLC has come grudgingly around to recognize its value. So much for the fear that we couldn't compete. We'd seen the same fears expressed in 1965 when we negotiated the first of the great modern free trade agreements, the Autopact. Auto parts continue to be our principal export to the United States.

What free trade has done is to create shared economic space in North America and the access has worked to Canada's advantage and that of the United States.

But for the United States, trade has always been coupled with security concerns. Canada looks south for economic reasons. America looks north and south, for security. The NAFTA was very much a strategic American policy aimed at curbing the increasing Mexican migration north by negotiating a trading framework that would establish the conditions for jobs and growth in Mexico.

Nine-Eleven changed everything. Security now trumps economics. Borders matter again. And the American model of border is one that they have had to maintain on their southern frontier. It is characterized by wires, walls and posses. I know, I've inspected the California border by hummer and helicopter.

We cannot have this model applied to our border. It simply wouldn't work. So what do we do?

The challenge is clear: we have to re-establish our credentials as 'with America on security'. We're not the trap door through which bad guys, B.C. bud and cheap drugs enter at will.

We have to do this to safeguard our economic access, which while we are mutually dependent is asymmetrical. America only sends us twenty-five per cent of its exports, we send them eighty-five per cent of our exports. Trade is much less important to the American economy: exports to Canada account for less than three per cent of their GDP, while over forty per cent of our own. In any debate in America security will always trump trade.

So what are we doing to convince America that we care and share the concern that "our security is indivisible", as Prime Minister Paul Martin put it?

First, we've negotiated the Smart Border Accord to secure and strengthen the passage of goods and people across our frontier. This means closer collaboration and joint customs inspection. It means using technology and risk-management. It means having American inspectors in Canadian ports and Canadian inspectors in American ports. We're experimenting with fast-passes for frequent travellers. It means moving the border beyond the border: bonding trucks as they leave their warehouse and then waving a wand as they cross the border in a fast-lane, to ensure seals are intact.

Second, we're reinforcing public security in intelligence and policy and the structures that support them. In the wake of 9/11, legislation was quickly passed (more quickly in Canada than in the United States) and implemented to more intensely screen immigrants and refugees and visitors. We're deporting those who shouldn't be here. We created the new Department of Public Safety and Emergency Preparedness, our version of Homeland Security, but with a more comprehensive mandate. It brings together the core functions of crime prevention, policing and enforcement, security and intelligence, corrections, border services and emergency management. At the end of April, Deputy Prime Minister Anne McLellan tabled the first Canadian comprehensive statement on national security and the prime minister has named Rob Wright, who headed our Customs Service, as our first National Security Advisor.

We've made progress — good progress. The border is more efficient, but we're not there yet. Crossing the border still involves delay and inconvenience. And there is American legislation on bio-terrorism and cargo supply where the penny is still to drop. The cost of complying with that legislation will be costly. Shippers are going to have to make buying, selling and shipping decisions earlier and get that information to border agencies before the truck arrives at the port of inspection.

It's obliging us to rethink borders and how we apply sovereignty. For example, if our customs and immigration stations have the same basic function, couldn't one do the job of the other? We've done air pre-clearance for fifty years at seven Canadian airports, surely we can create the legal regime that will respect mutual sovereignties but ensure mutual convenience.

Second, we're increasing our presence — we call it 'enhanced representation', from thirteen cities to forty-two. 'Being there', is essential to understanding the United States. 'Smart diplomacy' is the approach.

Small offices mean fewer people with focused activity. In Tucson, for example, we're renting space with the Greater Tucson Economic Council and our new officer spent the last five years with the University of Arizona working in life sciences — the area that he'll focus on. We're recruiting beyond the traditional foreign service. In San Jose, the head of our office comes from the Export Development Corporation. We're tapping our expatriates and making honorary consuls of these star-spangled Canadians. We'll bring in SWAT teams for big projects like Bio2004 in San Francisco.

At our Embassy in Washington we're establishing a Secretariat that will use the umbrella of the 'Canada brand' to more effectively advance our interests with Congress. The PM has invited the provinces to join the Secretariat. Premier Ralph Klein has already assigned an officer from Alberta. Premiers Doer, Campbell, Hamm and McGuinty have told me that they are giving it active consideration.

And we're going to use our elected officials and the special relationship they have as legislators, with fellow legislators in Congress and the state legislatures. We're building on existing relationships: the interparliamentary group of MPs and senators from our federal parliament and the relationships that already exist between premiers and governors and provincial and state legislators.

The Secretariat is a unique approach. No other country has anything like it. The premiers and parliamentarians have told me that their expectations from the Secretariat are threefold:

- Access through a network of contacts;

- An early warning system on emerging issues and trends;

- Advocacy capacity that will serve as both shield and sword.

They expect these objectives to be achieved through a 'Team Canada' approach drawing on the network of offices in the United States and in collaboration and cooperation with Headquarters, the provinces and legislators.

It's doing diplomacy differently. It's not incremental. It's pathbreaking in the same fashion we approached the FTA negotiations in the mid-eighties.

It's a partnership with the provinces. It builds on the relationship we developed during the trade negotiation of the FTA, NAFTA and at the WTO. At the end of March, for the first time, senior officers from the provinces participated in our planning exercise — determining what will be our objectives in the U.S. for this year. It's no surprise that at the top of the list were public advocacy and trade and investment development.

In practical terms, I see the Secretariat operating as a permanent 'war room'. Our job is to better advance Canadian interests, especially with

Congress. We will use our public diplomacy tools — public affairs, culture and relations with the learning communities, and align them to our congressional outreach team and apply the access afforded by our legislators.

My approach is this: preserve Canadian politeness but practise American forthrightness. Take risks. Don't let anything pass. Be in your face. In short, play the game the way Americans play it.

We've begun.

Two weeks ago a Democrat from Texas, in one of the salamander districts, got up in committee and proclaimed that "we all know the terrorists entered through Canada." As in the past we sent a corrective letter from Ambassador Kergin to the Congressman. But we did it the next day. And we also gave the letter to *Roll Call*, the daily newspaper of Capitol Hill. They would write a story about the "feisty Canadians". And we accomplished our point: we got our message out broadly.

Last Monday in the *Washington Times*, Canadian-born Hoover Fellow Arnold Beichman wrote that Canada was giving the cold-shoulder to America. By 6 p.m. we had a letter to the editor that we also copied to our Canadian watchers. It was brief, blunt and most importantly, in the same news cycle. This we have to do. But more, much more, remains to be done.

- First, and most importantly, we've got to know more about our interests in America so that we can use it as leverage with American legislators. We need to know, by congressional district, what America exports to Canada in goods and services. We need to know about Canadian investment in each district. We need to know the name of the company, its location and the number of people it employs.

As Tip O'Neill observed, "all politics is local". So when I go on the Hill or my colleagues at our offices in the states go talk with legislators, they will speak in the language that every legislator understand: jobs.

Towards this end, I am approaching the Canadian Chamber of Commerce, the Canadian Manufacturers and Exporters Association and the Canadian Council of Chief Executives, as well as other industry umbrella groups for beef and lumber. I want them to finance this study. And I'd like a consortium of universities and thinktanks, on both sides of the border, to do the research and keep it evergreen.

- Second, we need to know more about America. We think we know our neighbours, but do we really? Did you know that there is really only one centre of American studies in Canada. And, as they say on websites, it's 'under construction'. No other country is as well placed as Canada to interpret the United States. We share common economic space, we share a common language, we enjoy the same entertainment. My challenge is to Canadian universities to establish chairs and centres of American studies.

- Third, and this will be the biggest challenge: as a people, we need to cease defining ourselves by what we are 'not'. Too many Canadians when asked to describe what we are start with the negative: "we're not American." A people that defines themselves by what they are not and an identity that begins with the negative cannot inspire. We have to get past the assumption that we are somehow better than Americans. We are different. But we aren't better.

Unfortunately, we continue to leave the impression with our American cousins of the kind of attitude that led Dean Acheson to describe Canada as the "stern daughter of the voice of God". Or as Henry Kissinger put it a few weeks ago when I met him at the Republican National Convention: "Canada — Canada. I have dealt with Canada since Vietnam. The word that comes to mind when I think of Canada is 'self-righteous'. Yes, self-righteous. In Canada you get to do what is desirable. In America we must do what is necessary."

Insufferability is usually rooted in the insecurity of the mouse living next to the elephant. I think the analogy is wrong. We are not a mouse. We're a moose sharing space with the eagle. We are not American, but we are North American.

As Canadians we need to look through the right end of the telescope when we worry about 'our' cultural identity. By any American measure, by any world measure: the Oscars, the Emmys, the Grammies, the Pulitzers, the National Book Awards, Canada is a net producer of a North American culture of which we are an integrated and essential part. And we bring to them a lightness of touch: our sense of north, our sense of humour, our sense of people and place, that transcends borders.

Having spent a large part of my working career living beyond our borders I can tell you that the idea or 'brand' that Canada represents within North America and within the world is hugely envied. Every day that I am abroad, I meet people who want to come to Canada because of what that brand represents: freedom, cultural diversity, opportunity — values we share with our American cousins.

Our attraction and our strength are rooted in our diversity, a diversity constantly replenished by our open immigration. We are northern people:

the north of Hugh MacLennan, Glenn Gould, Roch Carrier, Robert Lepage, the Group of Seven. A Sense of North portrayed in films like *Atanarjuat, Men with Brooms, les Invasions barbares*. Storytellers like Rohinton Mistry, Carol Shields, Michael Ondaatje, whose tales are at once particular, yet universal, reflecting the impact of successive waves of immigration and the access that is open to all.

Climate and diversity has created a dynamic culture that becomes more original as we internalize diversity. Our culture is now characterized by both a 'diversity of authenticities' and an 'authenticity of diversity'. Without the awful baggage of ethnic or religious divide. We can actually inhabit the shoes of others. We are light on our feet. Our culture understands, preserves and integrates many cultures. And we do so with enormous success because we have a sensibility that travels well.

This sensibility and the commitment we make to learning more about America and our interests in America and the rest of the world, are means to an end. The end they serve is to give Canada the confidence and the knowledge to play an increasingly constructive role in the world.

- First, to defend and advance our own interests, especially with the United States.

- Second, to play the vital role of interpreter. To interpret the United States to the rest of the world. To interpret the rest of the world to the United States. This role is arguably even more valuable today than it ever was, as America rethinks and recalibrates its global involvement.

- Third, to make Canadian diplomacy, like our culture, an authentic Canadian medium that enriches our national life and, incidentally, makes a real contribution to international peace and security.

If the transatlantic world into which we are nestled, is coming undone, we have responsibilities. We have our interests, of course. But we shouldn't get too fixated on border, as important as it is. The Security Agenda is bigger, and it's spelled out in the U.S. administration's 2002 National Security Agenda. As for post-Iraq, what Bush 43 is doing is more likely to create a New World Order than what Bush 41 set out to achieve.

We face a real dilemma. Those who attack the UN and the multi-lateral system because it would outsource American foreign and security policy to a bunch of garlic-chewing, cheese-eating wimps are wrong-headed.

But it is also true that the cheese eaters need to set aside their Chateau Montrose and get real. The 'rules-based order' on which we correctly have placed such emphasis since WWII has always had a trap door for BIG states. The veto in the UN is the least of our worries — at least the U.S. is playing by the rules. Our challenge is to keep the rules-based system appealing enough that the 'hyperpower', and for the foreseeable future there is only one, doesn't take its marbles and go it alone.

As Canadians, as North Americans, we are uniquely placed to respond to these challenges. It requires leadership. It requires taking risks. It means doing things differently. But isn't that the definition of 'being Canadian'?

Working with America after 9/11

The Honourable Lloyd
Axworthy

Lloyd Axworthy is President and Vice Chancellor of the University of Winnipeg. Formerly Director and CEO of the Liu Institute for Global Issues at the University of British Columbia and Canada's Foreign Minister from 1995 to 2000, Lloyd Axworthy's political career spanned twenty-seven years, including six years in the Manitoba Legislature and twenty-one in the federal Parliament. In addition to Foreign Affairs, he also held five other ministerial portfolios.

As Minister of Foreign Affairs, Dr. Axworthy became internationally known for his advancement of the human security concept, in particular, the Ottawa Treaty — a landmark global treaty banning anti-personnel landmines. For his leadership, he was nominated for the Nobel Peace Prize. For his efforts in establishing the International Criminal Court and the Protocol on child soldiers, he received the North-South Institute's Peace Award.

Since leaving public life, he has also been the recipient of the Senator Patrick J. Leahy Award in recognition of his leadership in the effort to outlaw landmines and the use of children as soldiers, the Madison Medal from Princeton University for his record of outstanding public service and the CARE International Humanitarian Award. He has received nine honourary doctorates, was elected Honorary Fellow of the American Academy of Arts and Sciences, and has been named to the Order of Manitoba and the Order of Canada.

He graduated in 1961 with a B.A. from United College (now the University of Winnipeg), obtained his M.A. in Political Science from Princeton University in 1963 and a Ph.D. from Princeton in 1972. He remains involved in international matters and lectures widely in Canada, the U.S. and abroad. His book *Navigating a New World: Canada's Global Future*, was published in 2003.

In February 2004, UN Secretary General Kofi Annan appointed Lloyd Axworthy as his special envoy for Ethiopia-Eritrea to assist in implementing a peace agreement between the East African countries.

This paper is a revised edition of a lecture presented before an international audience in 2004.

2005

A New Court for a New Century

by Lloyd Axworthy

INTERNATIONAL DIPLOMACY is not usually seen as a joyous occupation. If economics is seen as the dismal science, then the world of international negotiation can be viewed as generally a grim, glum affair, only partially leavened by too many stuffy dinners and false expressions of bonhomie.

But once in a while there is a moment of exuberant glee, when the sheer delight at a surprise outcome after months, if not years, of hardscrabble work brings joy to the hardened heart.

Such a moment occurred just six years ago in a cavernous chamber on the outskirts of Rome when the International Criminal Court was born. Long will I recall the spontaneous outbreak of applause, cheering and — if you can imagine — hugging and backslapping as the results were read out reflecting an overwhelming confirmation for the treaty that would launch the twenty-first century's most important new global institution.

Later that night, as we sat in a Roman piazza listening in to the congratulatory call that our prime minister had placed to Phillipe Kirsch, chairman of the conference, the words of Dean Acheson came to mind — it was good to be in "at the creation".

It was for me an affirmation of two defining propositions and one compelling hope that I had carried in my political knapsack in those years at the Canadian foreign ministry — the belief that security had to be defined in terms of protection of individuals, the human security concept, that there was new diplomacy emerging that brought civil groups into partnership with like-minded countries to collaborate on creating new humanitarian norms and the practices and institutions to make the norms achievable.

And that out of the confluence of the two, it would be possible to truly anchor an international justice system that would offer an alternative to the realist, 'might makes right' school of diplomatic practice that I found to be so morally bankrupt. It would provide a way of dealing with the dark side, the underworld of globalism, the increasing threats from the international terrorists, pedophiles, drug dealers, small arms traders, illegal-diamond merchants and people smugglers. This underworld increasingly employs the tools of global networks of information, transportation, finance and organization, giving these predators the capacity to prey upon the vulnerable and establish international connections that are able to overwhelm the capability of individual nations to protect their citizens. Drug trafficking, for example, had become a multi-billion-dollar business netting annual profits that are greater than the GDPs of the majority of the world's nations.

Signing the treaty, of course, was only the beginning. It ushered in a very intense period of activity by a committed network of NGOs, governments, foundations, experts and international institutions to promote ratification, build the institution and carefully nurture the foundations of a fair, objective system of justice that could command respect and engender a sense of legitimacy — one of the high-water mark achievements as the new millennium took hold.

But then we entered what only can be called the dark ages — what Jane Jacobs describes as "a cultural collapse". Foundations of accepted wisdom and common practice were undermined and collapsed just as dramatically as were the concrete and girders of the Trade Center on September 11th. It became a time of terror and counter force, where all thought of human rights were put aside or at least shuffled to the back burner, and those of believing in the advancement of an international justice system were scoffed at by the new apostles of extremism and empire. We witnessed the transformative clash between two global networks: one of terror, unbound by territory, linked by thin tendrils of finance and communications, single-mindedly dedicated to the destruction of its enemy; the other centered in the world's most powerful state, but with spokes and connections encompassing powerful worldwide nodes of military, diplomatic and economic power.

The prevailing notion among the chattering classes was that we were entering a new age of unfathomable threat and the only way to meet such danger was through an empire based on massive overwhelming power, and we had better discard old-fashioned notions of rule of law and cooperative global action — it was our vale of tears. And nowhere was the issue more in doubt than in the case of the court that faced implacable opposition from the Bush administration and complicit retreat from other former advocates such as the Blair government and the Japanese.

But, history has a wonderful habit of playing jokes on politicians and academic sycophants alike; there just might be reason for a renewed sense of purpose and, if not the wild jubilation of six years ago, then grounds for prudent optimism. The post-Iraq war hangover may just be the harbinger of a rehabilitation of the concept of international justice as particularly relevant to the post-Iraq war period. It may fill the gap left by the U.S. come-uppance in Iraq, where its power could make easy pickings of the military campaign, but not in keeping the peace.

One thing that should be clear from any reading of history is that war always affects our rights and responsibilities as citizens; we can't escape the inexorable underlying shift in the power position of the state and those who control the machinery of war.

Equally, organizing the peace can rearrange relations between states and other international players. As Phillip Bobbit writes in *The Shield of Achilles*, "strategic imperatives animate constitutional innovation, questions of security yield new legal solutions, and require new stories to rationalize that solution." Climbing back from war and its aftermath needs guideposts, careful steering, a set of shared goals to reach. The post 9/11 world, the post-Iraq world cries out for such creative navigation. It cries out for a form of civility in global affairs, that sets rules, respects laws, gives protection to the vulnerable, encourages engagement and is inclusive in its reach — it is a call for global citizenship — and the establishment of an international justice system is one full expression of that principle.

The shock value of the revelations of the abuse of Iraqi prisoners at Abu Ghraib is also shifting the debate; the courts are being used to reassert prisoner rights. The decision by the International Joint Commission to rule an advisory against the building of the wall sets a standard that the international community must now consider. The inability of the United States to receive renewal of its exemption resolution (1452) at the Security Council is a portent of the altered state of global politics away from the assertive 'might makes right' crusade for dominance, of its right to forge a unidimensional approach, and the opportunity to offer an alternative effort. The show trial of Saddam Hussein by a court with no credibility is an object lesson on the stupidity of unrestrained power when contrasted to the recent decision of the chief justice of the Sierra Leone tribunal to excuse himself on potential grounds of bias, thereby setting a standard for fairness and objectivity that is emerging as a hallmark of the international justice system. The truly innovative developments in the treatment and compensation for victims and witnesses creates the foundation for a justice system in touch with the needs of the people, not the conquering power or the rapacious predators, and is a base for forging a form of loyalty and trust for justice among those who have been the violated.

So this may also be an occasion for some further celebration — that light is piercing the Dark Age. We may be in a position to draw forth the idea of an international justice system as a guidepost for the future. And just as in medieval times the construction of a soaring cathedral depended upon the craftsmen labouring to build a sure foundation, these early days have been constructive ones. I pay tribute to all those who have been keeping the flame alive and have persevered in constructing the court, choosing the justices, starting the investigations, pushing for further ratifications, organizing the administration and preparing the launch. Your work is also to be celebrated. And if, as promised by the prosecutor, the first investigation is to be formally initiated in the Congo and indictments laid, it will offer a visible sign of how to deal with criminals — in contrast to the victor's justice on display in Iraq.

There is therefore serious craftsmanship in building the system that must be further encouraged, in applying best practices — it's time therefore to recognize the continued need to support and refine the tools. I believe that the same coalition that created the court and carried it through the dark years must now reassemble to reach beyond the immediate and begin an active campaign to elaborate and communicate the larger vision for the court, which is the case for building an international justice system centered on the International Criminal Court.

It is a case that the ICC can become one of the most effective tools for combatting dictatorship, violations of individual rights and countering terrorism. It is the cornerstone for introducing into domestic legal systems the norms of the Rome Statute, and extending the reach of investigations and enforcement of criminal acts, including terrorists. It can have a major role in deterring criminal activity and therefore can supplement, perhaps supersede at times, the role of the UN in dealing with human security violations.

During a discussion with the highly respected UN ambassador from Jordan, Prince Zaid, who has played a critical role in guiding the establishment of the court through the UN process, he made the point that the ICC is the best embodiment of a smart sanction — targeting the perpetrators and not punishing the people, a realization that had been percolating with me since my first trip to the Balkans. I recognized then that we had to find a way of punishing the decision makers who cause the crime, not the people.

That the International Criminal Court can be the linchpin in developing an international criminal justice system is simple in its principle, but extraordinarily complex in its implementation. The efforts to create an environment where borders are no longer a shield from justice, have been threatened by defenders of the status quo.

And the case that the court can become the cornerstone of a global judicial system — incorporating international cooperation in investigation, forensic evidence gathering, police and enforcement action and prosecution, all done according to the precepts of respect for rights — has not been clearly seen, perceived or communicated. The use of human rights as a tool against the dark side of global society has not been advanced. The often favoured tool is the use of military arms, with limited and at times very damaging results. We are in a warrior mood in the West, and our public discourse is replete with calls to arms and recourse to military prowess to solve our security anxieties. Not that there aren't times when it may be necessary in order to enforce the rules of protection against those that would abuse them, but it is a means of last resort, and in itself must be accompanied by a healthy counterbalance against the capricious use of force in the hands of leaders. That is why the court must be put at the center of a global system of criminal justice, why it must be seen as a solution. The court's full potential can only be achieved if all states and all aspects of civil society understand and trust what the court exists to do, that it is an essential part of the effort for peace.

It's time to take the issue right to the very centre of the battle against terrorism and show that the ICC is one of the most effective and appropriate antidotes to the extreme acts of terrorist criminality, one that doesn't rely upon force of arms, but a clear and comprehensive legal and juridical system that can hold them to account, deter their action and extend the reach of law. It is the cornerstone for introducing into domestic legal systems the norms of the Rome Statute, using the Crimes against Humanity standards to go after the extremists who kill innocents to achieve their ends, and extending the reach of investigations and enforcement of these important additions to holding individuals accountable for crimes against their fellow citizens.

That's the potential; the key issue is to see the ICC not as just a court, but as a major way of internationally declaring the exercising of protection and prevention.

As John Lloyd wrote in the *Financial Times*, "Intervention has become a fact of life. Its future as international policy — and the future of the majority of the world's poor and struggling peoples — will depend on the articulation of rules and practices that command wider assent than at present."

Let me put this in the context of efforts to begin re-writing the elements of a new global definition to articulate those rules. One way is to begin seeing the court not just in its judicial, legal mode, but as a wider institutional effort to redefine the rights of the international community to intervene on behalf of individuals. As many know, I established a commission to come to grips with this issue following the Kosovo conflict. The commission has crafted a definition of sovereignty centered not on the prerogatives of the state, but on its primary responsibility to protect its citizens. If a state legitimately protects its citizens then it is in full right of its sovereign power. If it fails to do so, or in fact is the perpetrator of a massive attack on the rights of its citizens, then the international community must assume the function. To quote from the Core Principles set out in the Report:

> Where a population is suffering serious harm, as a result of internal war, insurgency, repression or state failure, and the state in question is unwilling or unable to halt or avert it, the principle of non-intervention yields to the international responsibility to protect.

This international responsibility breaks down into three specific tasks: prevention, reaction and rebuilding. The commission stresses that, "prevention options should always be exhausted before intervention is contemplated. And should always involve less intrusive measures before coercive measures are used." A high threshold must be met, such as large-scale loss of life or ethnic cleansing, before military action is warranted. Such intervention should be seen as a last resort and the minimum force necessary should be used to achieve the stated aim. The commission comes down squarely on the need to work through the Security Council, but suggests that the veto should not be used by the Permanent Five (P-5) unless their vital interests are at stake. If the council stalemates, there should be recourse to the General Assembly.

This is the gist of the report, with sovereignty seen not as a prerogative but as a responsibility. It is a way of coming at the tyrants who hide behind the walls of sovereignty.

There are a variety of efforts underway to create this new norm — at the UN, in regional organizations, as part of disarmament reform and in promoting environmental governance. All are increasingly holding individuals accountable for actions and justifying international preventative and pro-active actions. And right now, the court and the potential it poses for a broader global justice system is the most visible and illustrative of that alternative and therefore carries the greatest responsibility for acting as an anchor institution — the leading edge in forging an international system based on human security principles as expressed in the responsibility-to-protect concept.

This should be the rallying point for concerted, coherent political efforts by the human rights network — the combination of NGOs, like-minded governments, experts, international organizations: the human security group — to marry and wed together a campaign that combines the international justice prescriptions with the responsibility to protect, the idea being to offer a clear blueprint for dealing with today's security threats: the terrorist, the warlord, the trafficker. Let's call it the 'prevention, prosecution, and prescription' campaign (the 3P Program), designed to establish the rules of law and the means to enforce them based on mutual obligation and authority.

There are specific, immediate steps that must be part of the campaign:

1. Re-launch the universality campaign of ratification that has become stalled, beginning by calling for U.S. neutrality; in other words an end to the efforts to sabotage the court through the campaign of intimidation. As an aftermath of the Abu Ghraib scandal and the Supreme Court decisions on prisoners, there is a chance to remind Americans of the importance of the law and emphasize the complementary principle. To make this happen, European (and Canadian) leaders must be persuaded to make this a priority in re-establishing the elements of a transatlantic reconciliation. I would also suggest — perhaps for this meeting — a clearly articulated scenario of how the court can be an active player in the present genocidal crisis in Darfur in Sudan.

Perhaps this is the time to illustrate how the Security Council can use its reference power as a tool of deterrence. Bringing this power into play would further the case for relevance of the court. Along with being a potential deterrent to criminality and an instrument of justice, the ICC can also play the role of a powerful motivator for peace negotiations. This was evidenced in the former Yugoslavia, when within twenty-four hours of being indicted, a previously defiant Slobodan Milosovic was at the table, ready to negotiate.

2. There must be a major campaign to fully mobilize the human rights NGO community behind the ratification process and the domestic application of the Rome Statute. It was recently brought to my attention that the constituency of human rights groups now numbers in the vicinity of 25,000 worldwide — mostly at the local level. That shows remarkable growth and an even more powerful force to be mobilized. That is where the resources should be dedicated to creating a network behind the 3P Program, especially around the insertion of the Rome Statute as a fundamental element of their justice system, which creates ipso facto a global justice system. An international justice framework is unlikely to be sustained without corresponding national systems that are in harmony with and support international human rights. States that adjust their national laws to fulfill treaty responsibilities strengthen both domestic and international jurisprudence.

The ICC experience is a model of the significance of normative campaigns as a key strategy for enforcing human rights. The time is ripe for human rights activists and organizations to find new opportunities to move progressively ahead on establishing new standards to fit the changing context. If we simply dig in our heels to try to preserve the ground gained in the 1990s or become too involved in mechanics, we'll lose the chance to set bold new standards that I would argue are still very necessary, standards concerning the rights of non-citizens, the purveyors of weapons of mass destruction, or businesses that exploit resources. Major challenges exist in filling gaps in the rights architecture.

3. A key to establishing this role will be the way in which the ICC handles the delicate balance between justice and peace in its first cases in the Democratic Republic of the Congo and Uganda. This is the first time that there will be a major judicial intervention while a conflict is going on. It can have a powerful effect in protecting people by drawing attention to the conflict, by generating international response, by deterring further crimes and by compelling major reforms by government. In fact, it can point to major reforms of the statute itself by illustrating, as has ICC Chief Prosecutor Luis Ocampo, that the relationship between conflict and economic exploitation requires an amendment to include legal persons, not just individuals.

At the same time it raises deep concerns about the impact the indictments might have on hardening positions, making amnesty or local, tribal forms of reconciliation more difficult to apply. It's interesting that in the case of Uganda, the announcement of charges being laid took place while we were conveying the peace committee on a tour of world capitals;

there was discernible consternation in New York when the announcement was made. Later we arranged for the group to meet with Ocampo and assurances were given that the laying of charges would not deter the peace process — but a residual concern remains. It highlights the need to work with local populations, to not only be impartial but appear to be impartial, and to be timely and thorough in investigation. Most notably, bring to bear the provisions of the victims and witnesses unit to assure safety and eventually reparation, and develop, in consultation with the local community, the right mix of mechanisms and combination of international law and traditional justice mores to create a system tailored and compatible with tradition and custom. Here lies one of the most valuable contributions of the ICC, the broad concept of 'Responsibility to Protect' — the ability to demonstrate how justice can lead to a sustainable peace grounded in local agreement, acceptance and engagement.

The issue and the potential is well summarized by a recent report of the NGO, *Citizens for Global Solutions*, "The international community has a moral and political obligation i.e. responsibility to protect, to do more on all counts to resolve these conflicts. The ICC is one potential element of a solution. But its involvement raises a significant question: Will the ICC action help ameliorate these situations or only aggravate the conflicts?" The *Citizens for Global Solutions* concludes that if applied carefully and with full use of the victims and witnesses provisions, the ICC could play a useful role in furthering resolution of the conflicts, while laying the groundwork for long term reconciliation and stability.

4. Then there is the issue of enforcement. I had a meeting with Carla Ponti, the ICTY [the International Criminal Tribunal for Yugoslavia] prosecutor. Among her laments was the continuing liberty of [Bosnian Serb war leader Radovan] Karadzic and [army commander Ratko] Mladic and the seeming inability of NATO forces to bring them to justice. I later had occasion to raise the matter with senior officials at NATO, reminding them that one of the basic commitments in Kosovo was to promote justice. This was a failure at the same time that NATO is redefining itself as an out-of-area intervention force in Afghanistan and Iraq. It simply points to the lack of commitment and awareness of these officials in the police capacity to fulfill the justice responsibilities and the need to have a proper enforcement ability.

There can be no more important area of reform than to begin putting in place the capacity and the machinery to create a force that can act rapidly on behalf of the community of states as advocated in the Brahimi report.

If the objective is to protect people and prevent violence you send a legitimate credible UN presence to start a mission quickly — not wait for four to six months — then there is far less likelihood of people being murdered, or large scale massive ethnic cleansing. That suggests a dedicated UN mechanism or regional surrogates that would include a range of services — military, police and civilian, capable of using force even when opposed to it — an entity that can arrest and apprehend criminals and protect investigators, adding credibility to the international justice effort.

I want to mention the need to begin a major program of international justice and research, training a new cadre of lawyers, officials and experts, especially in those regions that lack capacity and resources. This is a pressing challenge for our universities and professional schools. Equally pressing is the need for serious inquiry into the future of international justice. I recognize there is already good research going on and more on the way, related to victims and witnesses procedures and other necessary analysis of what will be needed to make the court work . But beyond, as the institutions that constitute the skeleton of a future international justice system emerge and operate with increasing authority, basic questions will become ever more pressing: What are the relationships among the different parts? How do we connect traditional systems with the international codes and procedures? How can the system be sustained? What guarantees of recourse can be offered to those who need it? If there is to be a sustained and growing confidence in the courts, tribunals and procedures, then our international academic community must think systematically about the development of the international justice system.

Most of all, the movement must engage in a universal public education effort to inform and excite a generation about the possibilities of governing our global system in a more just and fair manner. This last year I travelled on a book tour in both the Canada and the United States. I detected a hunger for new forms of governance based on humanitarian values. I sense a broadly shared unease that our political system is not addressing that question with care or consideration.

Nowhere is this questing more apparent than in the disconnect felt with the political system by many. There is an undercurrent of concern that crucial issues are not being addressed, that in the name of security, facts are massaged to fit the agendas of those in power (witness the misinformation over weapons of mass destruction in Iraq), that it is difficult for individuals to have an influence, and that the impact of global forces cannot be managed in our domestically centered governance. In particular, I heard the lament that the tools we use to govern ourselves are less relevant to the intermingling of our common fate in today's global conditions. Many feel that our affairs are no longer governed or managed in a way that protects individuals against the impact of such global forces. Our understandable short-term preoccupation with security has obscured the vision of a world free from conflict. The word 'peace' is slipping from political discourse. But I also witnessed the surprise, particularly among young people, at discovering the exciting prospects offered by the court and the tribunals.

We are failing, however, to make full use of the powerful presence of the law in an effort to form a global citizenry. Without a substantial investment in global education we will not produce the level of involvement that is desired and needed. I've seen some remarkable examples of how information technology opens up an incalculable number of educational opportunities. Some examples: the Grade 7 children in a school in Winnipeg who are connecting with their fellow students in Mexico to plan a campaign to save the monarch butterfly; the young people at a war children's conference in Accra explaining their circumstances to a group of high-school students in Canada; the Youth Links project that hooks up young people in great Britain and Canada to engage in a mutual education about each other's countries; the virtual Arctic University that will link students in eighteen educational institutions in eight circumpolar countries to share a course on arctic studies. All these and many more equally compelling demonstrations show the potential to break down barriers, overcome differences, and provide a shared multicultural perspective and understanding on global issues. Yet, despite all the pilot projects and individual initiatives, the effort to construct a comprehensive network for global-based education is spotty, fragmented and under-funded. A functioning fair system of laws cannot be sustained without public support.

The trials of Slobodan Milosevic and Saddam Hussein and all the other tyrants offer a moral object lesson on the powerful impact that a justice system can have in shaping views towards a different future. Writing in the *The Times* of London recently, Simon Sebag Montefiore caught just how important the courts can be in addressing our contemporary ferment:

> These trials are acts of remembrance; demonstrations that leaders are responsible for their crimes, and exhibitions of true justice. They are both a healing tonic

and a lesson not from history but from today, delivering repentance, redemption and renaissance. Combine this with the potential to demonstrate a degree of comprehensive justice as exemplified by the new approaches to victims and witnesses and you have an opportunity to engage the support and commitment of ordinary people around the world, who will see that it is a system designed for the forgotten and the abused. This in itself creates a powerful force of opinion and behavior that can only lift the level of global citizenship.

Renaissance — that should be the spirit that dominates and informs these proceedings — emerging from a dark period, seeing light ahead, setting a strong and steady course with eyes set towards a far horizon. This truly is a time to celebrate the possibilities that lie ahead. As Graham Greene has written, "Once in a while a door opens and lets the future in." This is such a moment. It is time to follow the old Roman dictum, *carpe diem* — seize the day.